Route 66

Photographs and stories from the Mother Road

Text and Photography by David Schneider

ISBN: 978-0-9838967-6-0

Route 66: Stories from the Mother Road © 2018 by David Schneider. All rights reserved.

Text and Photography by David Schneider

Edited by Bobbie Christmas

Created, produced, designed, and printed in the United States

No part of this publication may be reproduced, stored in a retrieval system, or transmitted in any form or by any means, electronic, mechanical, photocopying, recording, or otherwise (except for the purpose of review) without the prior written permission of the publisher.

An imprint of Fringe Innovations

For more information about our books, write Fringe Publishing, PO Box 555, Tijeras, NM 87059, call (505) 750-4PIX, or visit www.fringepublishing.com

Contents

Introduction	1
Illinois	5
Missouri	21
Kansas	35
Oklahoma	39
Texas	55
New Mexico	63
Arizona	77
California	91
Epilogue	101
About David	105

Introduction

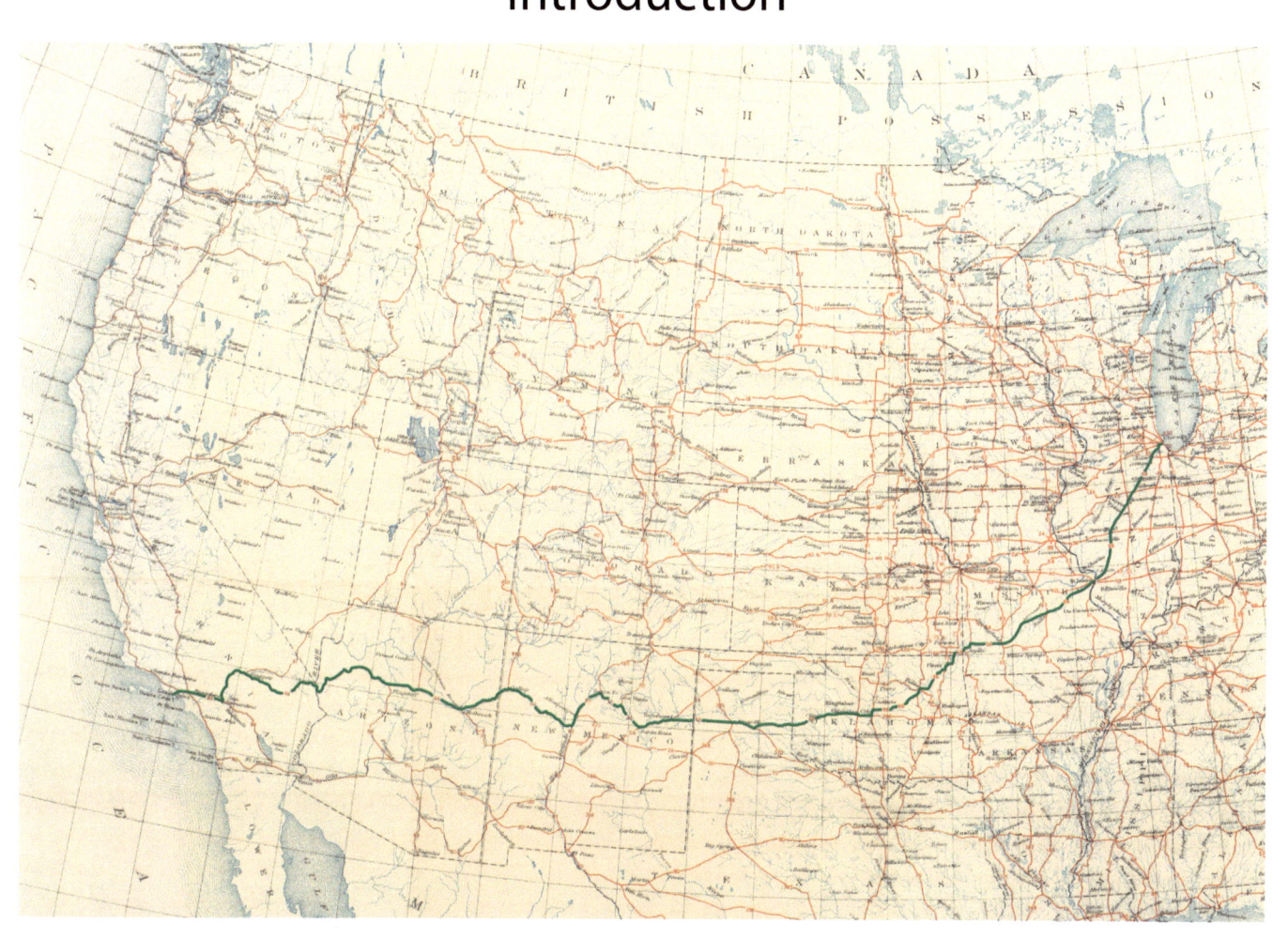

The dream of the open road has been with us since the advent of the horseless carriage, a vision that continues with us today. Slipping behind the wheel, bringing our car to life, and becoming one with the highway, wherever it shall lead, is a familiar motif. We memorialize highway adventures in song, deed, and legend. We write stories and create movies about such journeys, we fantasize about them, and the highway is part and parcel of our culture. The open road has always been an allure to us, an invitation to drive, experiencing the thrill and the joy of where it leads us.

After automobiles gained popularity, paved streets followed, and eventually the United States Numbered Highway System efficiently guided people to where they needed to go. Using these nationally designated and importantly, numbered, routes motorists could quickly plot a long trip. These numbered routes opened up whole new vistas for drivers and became incredibly popular. The routes represented progress, progress that was glorious for the motorist. On November 11, 1926, the most famous route of all, Route 66, was formally designated, and the Mother Road was born.

Route 66 became the Main Street of America. Full of the best that America had to offer, Route 66 delivered astounding experiences. The road was full of colorful signs advertising colorful places. As day metamorphosed into night, the Mother Road transformed into a necklace of neon, each sign trying to outshine the one before it, and in many cases, succeeding. Gas stations, diners, motor courts, motels, trading posts, and more dotted the roadside. You could stay in a teepee at night and have breakfast in a Valentine Diner the next morning. You could swim with a brightly colored blue whale, or you could see the biggest rattlesnakes known, if you were inclined to believe the sign. You could find treasures unheard of at the trading posts, and you could see sights such as leaning water towers placed along the road to lure you in. Along the way you could fill up at any of the countless gas stations, all with attentive attendants. It was, after all, The Mother Road. Alas, progress continued.

Today when we need to drive a long distance, and often even a short one, we use the current interstate system. We merge onto at least a four-lane divided highway and whiz across town, or the entire country, arriving, we hope, unhindered by traffic, at our destination. The interstate propels us countrywide at a constant, fast speed. We traverse hill, river, and dale without slowing down. With the help of tunnels and tall bridges we zip straight through mountains and across the highest gorges without a second thought. No obstacle was too great for the interstate system to overcome, leaving us with a glistening strip of high-speed asphalt from coast to coast. We hum along paying scant attention to the sights just off the highway, looking for our exit. Once there, we dart off, having arrived in the least amount of time possible.

The interstate system, in the interest of speed and efficiency, passed through many cities and towns yet skipped others. Those bypassed felt the impact of decreased traffic resulting in fewer customers at businesses. Bypassed areas, no longer vibrant and bustling, struggled to thrive and even survive. The streets through these towns grew emptier, even as more travelers than ever cruised the interstates. Gas stations, restaurants, motels, and other businesses that lined the older streets all closed their doors. The smaller towns suffered the greatest impact and faced an existential crisis, while the larger cities experienced a different effect. The interstates poured more travelers into these towns, but along the former, and now slower, Route 66, businesses faced the same problem as in smaller towns. The impact of America's changing highways was profound.

The consequences for the Mother Road as a whole were deep, profound, and near fatal. No longer did we think of it as the only way to travel from Chicago to Los Angeles. Now we can easily fly or use the interstate, trimming a journey that could last weeks to a couple of days or mere hours. No longer did we travel through the necklace of neon lights across America, and we no longer thought about the small towns that warranted at best only an exit sign. Today we zoom by Dwight, Cuba, Baxter Springs, Stroud, Vega, Tucumcari, Oatman, and Needles without slowing down, or worse, even noticing they exist.

One by one the neon signs failed to light at night, and little by little the Open signs were never turned on in the morning. Piece by piece America's Main Street diminished. As each business shuttered its doors, one more bit of the Mother Road faded away. Entire towns ceased to exist, sliding into the eternal abyss of progress.

Route 66 was the Main Street of America, however. Even though many of the icons faded and others disappeared entirely, Route 66 lives on. Route 66 still sees travelers who want to experience the Mother Road. Scattered here and there some pockets are still alive, bright and vibrant. You can still spend the night in a teepee or a motor court. You can still eat breakfast at a diner. You can still see a few neon signs at night, holding out against the darkness, beckoning you. You can still stop at a trading post, although seeing a live rattlesnake is no longer possible. You can still swim with the Blue Whale, and you can still experience Main Street as it once was. The smaller towns, especially, have embraced Route 66 and their place on it, keeping the spirit alive.

Route 66 takes us the length of the highway, from Chicago to Los Angeles. Along the way we'll experience the road as it always has been. We'll also see some of the classic icons before they fade away. At times a joyful journey, and at times merely a reminder of a time now passed, *Route 66* delivers The Mother Road experience.

It is tempting to think of Route 66 as a single road stretching from Chicago to Santa Monica, and in concept, it certainly is. In actuality, however, the official route has changed, sometimes considerably, over the years, especially in the earlier years. Sometimes this change was merely a block or two in a town, but sometimes it was far more significant, downturning the fortunes of the bypassed cities and spurning the fortunes of towns on the new official route. *Route 66* follows the route as it was in the 1940s and 1950s, although now and then we take a small detour onto an earlier alignment.

All the photographs in *Route 66* were made on Route 66, and I mean "made on Route 66" in the most literal sense. If my feet were not on Route 66 or the property didn't touch Route 66, I did not include it. Throughout this journey, I saw many opportunities to step off the route, even by a block or two, for many impressive sights, but for purposes of this book you and I will restrain ourselves to our goal of traveling only Route 66. While we're at it, we'll also note that some of the photographs were "rolled back" to an earlier time. Items such as telephone poles, modern-day signs, and other minor details were removed from the photographs. Nothing is more disheartening than finding the perfect sign you have been searching for in the last thousand miles, only to find it obscured by a stray electrical wire, so in some instances I rolled the image back to the appropriate year.

I've researched Route 66 extensively. Information in this book comes from historical markers, signs, plaques, field notes, long-forgotten tomes, and especially the people who live and work along the route. A surprising amount of information is out there on the route and a surprising amount promptly contradicts the last piece you just found.

Whenever possible I talked with whoever didn't run away from me and listened to their stories. As a result I've likely heard a tall tale or two that I didn't know was a tall tale. And a couple of times I was told a really tall tale, but at least I didn't fall for it right then and there. Usually. Where necessary, I've read old documents such as highway guides and protocols, historical commentary, newspaper articles, and a few ancient and largely out-of-print books. You would be surprised what you can find in a book about highway signs used for advertising purposes. The National Park Service and its Corridor Preservation Program is another surprising source of information, most of which is accurate. I've tried to recall and cross-check my notes as best as possible, but if I misrepresented a property, please let me know so I can correct it in a future edition. If I've missed an amazing story, I also hope you'll contact me so I can include it. Because these stories are people-based, however, some errors and omissions are bound to happen.

Let's start our journey down the Mother Road, Route 66.

Illinois

We start our journey on Route 66 in Illinois from downtown Chicago. We make our way out of the city and into the rolling countryside. We get our first glimpse of the open road, and we are officially on our way. We are now Santa Monica bound!

Route 66 officially begins at the intersection of Michigan Avenue and Adams Street in downtown Chicago, directly across from The Art Institute of Chicago. Chicago has changed over the years, so the original route bears little resemblance to what it was. In fact the only real marker is a single Begin Historic 66 sign on a lamp pole. It may be a modest beginning for such an intrepid road, but it is our beginning nonetheless. From here we head due west, making our way through the city and its numerous suburbs.

Route 66 through Chicagoland, just as in so many other places, has mostly either been swallowed up by the growing city or faded away. One small pocket remains, Dell Rhea's Chicken Basket. Dell Rhea's has been serving travelers since 1946. As you look around, you can find no trace of Route 66; the area now hosts light industry.

Dell Rhea's keeps up the tradition, still a must-stop location on the way into southern Illinois. Besides, its chicken is delicious! Leaving Dell Rhea's, we follow the old route, but that's all we are doing, just following where it used to be. Our adventure will renew once we depart the Chicago suburbs.

As we leave Chicagoland and reach the countryside, we experience the open road for the first time. No longer hemmed in by the sprawling metropolis, we see for miles ahead of us down the two-lane highway. To the left and right, farmers work their fields, and what traffic there is appears only in our rearview mirror. From here until St. Louis, we encounter only small towns, with each patiently waiting for us to stop at their businesses. Not all places are content merely waiting, however; some help us find them by any number of means.

The Launching Pad in Wilmington is one of those cases. In the 1960s, this restaurant decided that a thirty-foot-tall statue of a spaceman holding a rocket, known as the Gemini Giant, would draw attention, which would, in turn, cause people to stop and have a meal. A thirty-foot-statue does indeed get noticed. The Gemini Giant is not the only giant used for advertising. In the 1960s a few of these giants were scattered across the country, although all but a few have vanished. It is delightful that we can see one still in use.

A few miles farther along, we come to the small town of Braidwood and notably The Polk-A-Dot Drive-In. In business since 1956, The Polka-A-Dot is still faithful to its roots as a drive-in restaurant.

Over the years, The Polk-A-Dot Drive-In has picked up a bit of a retro theme and quite the collection of memorabilia. As wonderful as the classic diner is, at the back of it is an ancient stoplight and faded US Route 66 sign. It is impossible to know where these items came from, but you can bet that more than a few travelers once stared at the red light willing it to quickly turn green. Today it doesn't turn any color but is an excellent reminder of past days.

As we travel through Gardner, Illinois, we'll find the 1932 Streetcar Diner. Once a horse-drawn Kankakee streetcar, it was later converted into a diner. Interestingly, this small eatery sat in the back of a far more famous one, the Rivera Roadhouse. The Rivera Roadhouse was a favorite stop, and the nearby diner was paid scant attention, at least until a suspicious fire burned down the Rivera Roadhouse in 2010. In memory of the Rivera, the Streetcar Diner was lovingly restored and then moved to a small park, where it stands today. Although it stopped serving diners quite some time ago, it still provides a testament to Gardner's place on the Mother Road.

Dwight, Illinois, has one of the better-preserved gas stations in Illinois, the Ambler-Becker Texaco Station. Initially serving Dwight in 1933 under the Texaco brand, this cottage-style station also served Marathon. It underwent many changes and additions over the years and eventually grew into two bays and five pumps, operating as a gas station until 1999. From 1999 until 2002 it was an auto repair station, at which time the owner donated the property to the village of Dwight. From there, restoration efforts returned it to a 1930s/1940s appearance, which we see in this photograph, and it now operates as Dwight's visitor center.

This close-up captures one of the pumps at the Ambler station. The gas price, which would be wonderful to have today, is 23-9/10 cents per gallon. The signage here claims that the station had the last working gas pumps on the Mother Road from Illinois to California, but perhaps the signs mean these were the last gas pumps from the 1960s style, or perhaps the last Marathon ones. Either way, the station operated continuously from 1933 until 1999, an impressive achievement.

This Mobil station lies in the middle of Odell. The two-bay structure, long out of service, has two vintage cars sitting next to it, giving the illusion that it might still be in business. The design of the station is from the 1950s, although today it is privately owned by a resident.

You can find small pieces and symbols of Americana in the most out-of-the-way places if only you look. The faded Coca-Cola sign is on the side of the Mobil station. You have to carefully look for this one, but set against the faded red wood it makes a fabulous photograph.

Iliinois 9

The front of the station reminds us in no uncertain terms that better days have long gone. All that remain are the empty oil rack and an old pump; however, Mobil's signature Pegasus is in good shape. The winged Pegasus has been a trademark since Magnolia Petroleum used it in the 1930s. Farther down the road, we'll see a restored Magnolia station and chat a bit about its history.

In 1932 Patrick O'Donnell built a small gas station along Route 66 in Odell and sold Standard Oil gasoline. The station was a favorite stop, and it did well for itself over the years. As frequently happened with the smaller filling stations, it switched brands, becoming a Sinclair and later a Phillips 66. Like Ambler's, two bays were added to the station, also making it a full-service station. Repair services, as it turned out, were becoming a necessary feature of the stations, and across the country many expanded and upgraded. For years we associated gasoline and repairs together, although in present times the two are once again separating.

The Odell Station didn't fare as well as Ambler's, and its pumps stopped in the 1960s. From there, it mostly drifted in purpose, finally becoming an auto repair station until it closed in 1999. Like nearby Dwight, the village of Odell purchased the station and restored it, bringing it back to an early 1940s appearance. The gas station is well preserved and once again sees plenty of visitors.

The Odell gas station is an excellent illustration of what happens when a town, and thus the station, is bypassed. The station did well in the early days when Route 66 went through town; however, in the 1940s a bypass was built around Odell, which dramatically hurt the station's business. When the interstate opened in the 1960s, it marked the end of the station. It certainly wasn't alone in its struggles, and luckily, the town stepped in to preserve and maintain its history.

Just outside of Cayuga we find the first, and one of the oldest, examples of barn advertising for Missouri's Meramec Caverns.

When you cruise down the highway in Illinois, there isn't a lot to keep your attention. The countryside is lovely, to be sure, but mile after mile of fields and barns tend to blur together. Lester Dill, who owned Meramec Caverns, found a way to break up the monotony with the simple solution of painting advertisements for his caverns on barns. He used this simple yet highly effective technique extensively on Route 66. Today only a couple barn advertisements remain, this being one of them. Luckily it was restored in 1998, giving us an excellent view of this iconic advertisement.

Outside of Pontiac we encounter the old District 6 State Police Headquarters. Constructed in 1941 using the Art Moderne style, it saw service until 2003, while officers used this building as their headquarters. Glass and long lines gave the building its distinctive look.

Fittingly, the old pavement runs right in front of the building, letting officers get quickly to the scene. We will reencounter the law a little later in our journey.

Memory Lane, as it is known today, is located on the outskirts of Lexington. This one-mile strip of original 1926 pavement protects and preserves the memory of Route 66 in Illinois. Usually closed to vehicles, it serves as a reminder of the days gone by, and importantly gives you a feel of how it was to drive on the original route. You might be tempted to think that all of Illinois winds through shady trees, but don't be fooled. Illinois is mostly flat farmland. This strip is an exception, but all the more beautiful because of it.

Long before the interstates and their exit signs, small towns often used signs of their own to announce their presence to travelers. Lexington, Illinois, was no exception, and this sign let motorists know where they were. It helpfully has an arrow, but it isn't needed, since Lexington is and always has been fairly small and compact. Further, this sign's location is almost halfway through Lexington. Still, it is a classic Route 66 sign.

Dead Man's Curve is a term long used when referring to very sharp turns, and it is only fitting that Route 66 has two. The first we encounter is in Towanda, Illinois, on a long-bypassed segment. This curve is certainly sharp and was the cause of many an accident as unsuspecting motorists sped around it.

Installed around the curve for you to read, as if you didn't already enough demands on your attention while navigating it, are a set of Burma Shave signs. These signs are part of one of the most famous advertising gimmicks ever created. In the mid-1920s a small company called Burma Shave came up with a unique way to advertise its shaving products: small

sequential signs alongside the road. Typically the six signs each featured one short line of poetry and the last sign said Burma Shave. These signs were an instant hit and largely contributed to Burma Shave's success.

Forty-five of the forty-eight contiguous United States contained Burma Shave signs, so saying they were everywhere is an understatement. Almost all the signs had white letters on a red background, and the poetry ranged from whimsical to macabre. The concept was so successful, in fact, that even today we recognize it, and from time to time a company still uses the idea. It became a part of American history and culture.

When Phillip Morris acquired Burma Shave in 1963, the signs began disappearing from the roadways, and today the original signs are long gone. Now and then, however, we can find re-creations of them, like this set.

This lovely set contains just five signs instead of the usual six, but since we are here, we'll include them. You don't even have to slow down to read them, but then you might discover why locals call this curve Dead Man's Curve.

Sprague's Super Service is newly restored to the way this impressive station used to be. Located in Normal, Illinois, the imposing station is located in a neighborhood, just as many of these early filling stations were. Like others, it architecturally attempted to blend in with the surroundings and project a trustworthy feel by using a cottage design. For the longest time this station sat decaying, but thanks to a multi-year restoration effort, we can once again stop here and fill up. Well, we could if the pumps were working, but we can still fill up on stories of the Mother Road and memorabilia from the gift shop inside.

Not far south of Bloomington is Funks Grove. Long bypassed, the small community continues, paying little attention to the outside march of time. Notably, though, Funks Grove is home to Funks Grove Pure Maple Sirup. The colorful chairs invite the traveler to sit, rest, and visit awhile, but these will not be the last chairs that catch our attention.

Now that we've worked up an appetite, we'll visit the Cozy Drive-In in Springfield. Serving Cozy Dogs, hot dogs coated in batter, the Cozy Drive-In has long been a favorite of everyone who stops here, and truly the Cozy Dog is something different. Also different is the charming logo of two hot dogs in an embrace. Although not a neon sign, it will still bring a smile to your heart. It is the only logo like it on the Mother Road.

One of the neatest sections of Route 66 is just outside of the small city of Auburn and covered in bricks. Most of the original roadbed was Portland Concrete, some of which is accessible today. Usually when the road was improved it was covered with a layer of asphalt, a practice that continues. Here, though, bricks were used as the overlay, and remarkably, they remain in place, still carrying traffic. A 1930 realignment of Route 66 bypassed this portion, which possibly saved this section from being paved over in later years.

You would expect a bumpy ride on the Auburn Brick Road, but it is remarkably smooth. In just a short distance you're completely used to it, and when you reach modern pavement and the bricks fade back into the past, you miss them. Here and there you'll find inevitable potholes, but the highway department fixes these issues with more bricks, keeping this section in character and pristine.

All in all, the Auburn Brick Road is a unique and enjoyable segment of the Mother Road.

The Ariston Café in Litchfield is a success story. When it opened its doors in the current location in 1935, it could have hardly imagined the stories it would see and how long it would remain open. The café claims to be the longest-running restaurant on Route 66. The original Ariston Café opened in 1924 in Carlinville, but when the owner saw that Route 66 routed through Litchfield, he moved to this location, an action that turned out to be wise and prescient.

Although built in the 1930s, the building doesn't sport the typical art deco styling of the time. It has a more utilitarian design, which suits the building well. Moreover, the bright neon sign tells us it is open and serving delicious meals.

Iliinois 15

Sometimes only small pieces of Route 66 have survived, somehow escaping demolition. The Vic Suhling Gas For Less sign, directly across the street from the Ariston Café, is a perfect example. The sign is the only remnant of a gas station that once stood here. This recently restored sign remains a beacon, although if you need fuel, you will need to look elsewhere.

Now and then a small part of Route 66 appears in the seemingly most unlikely places. Soulsby Station in Mount Olive is one of those locations. Constructed in 1926, this station served travelers until 1991, when it finally closed. The fully restored station looks precisely the same as it did back in the day, and when you come across it, it is easy to forget what year it is.

This station, like so many others in this area of the country, were located in neighborhoods, which today seems odd to us. When traveling the interstate, we're used to exiting at the next off-ramp and pulling into a large gas station often serving automobiles as well as large trucks. There will be plenty of pumps, quite probably a restaurant, and a convenience store, all of which are expedient, and all of which help us forget how things used to be.

These small cottage-style stations were not run by large corporations, but by individuals and their families, often handed down from father to son. In those days uniformed attendants rushed out to fill your gas tank, wash your windshield, and check your oil. The stations themselves, an integral part of their neighborhoods, blended in with their surroundings harmoniously. The pitched roofs on the overhangs were designed to give a comforting and trusting feel by vaguely reminding you of home, and being in a neighborhood heightened that perception.

Unlike many of the stations, this one remained branded to a single oil company—Shell. The last recorded price on the gas pumps is 33-9/10 cents a gallon, which makes you wish you could fill up here.

In Staunton, Illinois, we find a semi-truck trailer from Campbell 66 Express at Henry's Rabbit Ranch. We might not think it is a big deal, but it is significant for a few reasons.

Typically when we think of the Mother Road, we reminisce perhaps of a convertible with its top down cruising down the highway without a care in the world. Maybe we think fondly back to family vacations on the road or we have other sentimental memories, most of which involve an automobile. Route 66 was important for the trucking industry, too, since trucks used it extensively to move goods across America. The trucks used the US Routes whenever they could, and you found semis everywhere you went. Even the early postcards often had a semi truck on them, all of which brings us to Campbell 66 Express.

Campbell 66 Express was a Midwest trucking line that operated from 1933 to 1986. Back in the early days of trucking, the industry was tightly regulated, making it difficult at best for new truck lines to establish themselves. Existing carriers like Campbell grew large, and in so doing, their trucks, and trailers were everywhere.

What makes Campbell 66 Express trucks easy to recognize is the running camel logo, pictured on the trailer above, and its unusual slogan "Humpin' to Please." You couldn't help smiling or even laughing when you saw one of its trailers.

Campbell is also significant because its logo is a camel, and as we shall see later, there is a genuine connection between Route 66 and camels, of all animals. We'll see the camel motif a few more times.

As a bit of trivia, each Campbell 66 Express camel logo was hand painted by Bill Boyd. He painted a lot of logos.

The Kaiser Frazer sign in Edwardsville has seen better days and hangs on by a thread. The other side has been crudely painted over for the Town & Country Motel. It won't be long before the sign will be gone, and this site will only exist in memory.

The Bel Air Drive-In theater in Granite City hasn't shown a movie since 1986. Once part of a two-screen drive-in, the Bel Air was the spot to be on a Saturday night. The Bel Air faced, and succumbed to, the double threat of a fading Route 66 and the decline in drive-in movie theaters. It didn't stand much of a chance to stay in business, yet it won't be the last drive-in we encounter on our journey.

The Greenway Motel in Granite City was a late holdout, remaining open long after the other motels in the area had shut down. The last guest checked out long ago, though, and it has begun its decline into history.

As we head out of Illinois we come to the magnificent Chain of Rocks Bridge. Spanning the mighty Mississippi River, this 5,353-foot bridge first opened to traffic in 1929. Originally it was intended to go straight across the river, but that plan changed quickly because a straight bridge would place it too close to the water inlets for the Chain of Rocks Pumping Station and take it over an area of the riverbed not stable enough to support the piers. The solution was a unique thirty-degree bend partway over the river, giving the bridge its distinctive appearance.

Route 66 was officially rerouted over the bridge in 1936, making not only a major river crossing but also a destination in itself. This tremendous engineering feat was a pleasure to visit and drive. Progress, however, in the form of Interstate 270, happened within sight of the Chain of Rocks Bridge, and in 1968 the bridge was officially decommissioned. The bridge was scheduled to be demolished and would have been, if the price of scrap metal had been higher than the demolition cost. Luckily for us the bridge has been preserved as is, giving us a glimpse of what it was like back in the day.

Partway over the bridge, just before the bend, you cross the state line, leaving Illinois. We're now in Missouri

Missouri

We cross the mighty Mississippi River and continue our journey. We are now truly westward bound. The road continues ahead of us, across gentle and rolling hills, through woods, and over small rivers, smooth as can be.

St. Louis is the largest city on Route 66 between Chicago and Los Angeles, and it is a major stopping point. Heady travelers had just crossed the Mississippi River, and there, before them, an entire city awaited. Route 66 wound through St. Louis, and as expected, St. Louis did not disappoint. Like in the larger cities, though, Route 66 was quickly consumed by progress, and fewer landmarks remain, but a couple need mention.

No trip through St. Louis, no matter what year it is, would be complete without a stop at Ted Drewes for its frozen custard. Ted Drewes has been serving custard since 1929 and has had a location on Route 66 since 1941. Ted Drewes had and still has a nearly cult-like following, and people come from miles away to enjoy the custard. Although some businesses have struggled on Route 66, Ted Drewes is not among them.

Frozen custard is, of course, not the only treat and diversion available to the traveler. Another popular pastime is bowling, and what better place than the lanes at Crestwood Bowl in St. Louis?

When Route 66 was in its heyday, Crestwood Bowl shone brightly. In 1958 bowling was popular, with bowling teams were hitting their stride and becoming household names. Often breweries sponsored a team, a natural fit.

For the Route 66 travelers, Crestwood Bowl was within easy distance of their motel and offered an entertaining evening's diversion.

Leaving St. Louis, we once again pick up the feel of the open road. The sights, sounds, lights, and congestion of the big city fade away, replaced by grass at the sides of the road and trees beyond that. The fact that we have left St. Louis behind, however, doesn't mean we have to leave the comforts of Route 66 behind. The Gardenway Motel in Villa Ridge was there, lights on, with rooms available for us. Built in 1945, it stayed open for almost seventy years, finally closing in 2014. While still operating, its neon sign and bright letters spelling out Gardenway on top of the motel could be seen for quite a way, encouraging weary travelers to spend the night, and many did.

The Sunrise Motel, properly in Villa Ridge, left absolutely no doubt about where the entrance and exit was.

Sometimes a destination became popular because it was at the right place with the right traffic, and people naturally stopped there. On the other hand some cafés and motels needed a colorful neon sign to help people find them. Some attractions like Meramec Caverns, however, took advertising to a whole new level.

It was hard to travel within a thousand miles of Meramec Caverns without finding a billboard for it. The abundant Meramec billboards were placed up and down the highway, often right next to each other.

Most were unique, although now and then you would see a duplicate. In any event, the billboards made a statement and an impact, and most of all, they worked. The closer you were to the caverns, the more billboards you would find, and by the time you were approaching Meramec Caverns, you were happy to spend some time there, if for no other reason to than to escape the billboards.

Some motels along the way naturally stand out, as is the case with the Wagon Wheel Motel in Cuba. The Wagon Wheel features a western theme, even this far east, and its quaint stone cottages are made entirely of rock. When it was in full operation, it also featured a café and a gasoline station, making it a coveted one-stop shop for any need. The motel booked its first rooms in 1935 and is still open for business today, a testament to its outstanding reputation on the highway. Throughout its long history, it has seen upgrades and additions, making this icon of Route 66 one of continuous change and improvements.

Just before you reach Rolla, there is the Route 66 Motors Nostalgia and Gift Shop. This store has an extensive collection of old signs collected from, well, everywhere. We'll include these signs since the shop was open in 1979 and saw traffic from the Mother Road.

As we arrive in Rolla, we find the Mule Trading Post and its wonderful hillbilly sign, which demands attention. Originally opened in 1946, the Mule Trading Post relocated to this location in 1957. Here it was able to take advantage of both Route 66 and the new Interstate 44, the latter built on top of the former. Either way, the Mule made a success of it, in no small part due to the hillbilly sign.

The goal of any sign is to announce and advertise a business, ideally attracting people to it. This sign does all that and more. It makes you sit up and pay attention, and it is nearly impossible to drive by it without stopping to see what the Mule is all about. The hillbilly sign was originally part of the Sterling Hillbilly Store in Hooker, Missouri, but it has become part of Route 66 lore and legend simply by being itself.

Other signs, like the Totem Pole on the other side of Rolla, don't miss a chance to add a little bit extra. We can get everything we need and want here: gasoline, fireworks, moccasins, T-shirts, and more. Best of all, according to the sign, it is the "oldest since 1933," although it doesn't specify what the "oldest" is.

Missouri 25

When you are hungry for a cookie, look no farther than your nearest Dairy King. Dairy Kings are more famous for their highway-shield-shaped cookies than anything else, which is not at all what you would expect from a sign with the word "dairy" in it. Luckily they also sell ice cream. Although not many Dairy Kings remain, they are still a welcome sight, and tasty, too, when you find one.

For most of the route, the highway is a two-lane affair, and in the early days, it was made of Portland Concrete. Some cities had more than two lanes, but this was not a common occurrence. Hooker Cut is a large exception to this generality.

This 1940s alignment was built to bypass a previous, more dangerous alignment. In a rare case of earth moving, engineers dug ninety feet to create the highway. Given that Route 66, as all US Routes, followed the contours of the land, digging out ninety feet was a big deal. The four lanes were needed at the time to move military traffic from nearby Fort Leonard Wood. Remarkably the original four-lane Portland Concrete remains in pristine condition today.

Although the Big Piney River guards the way into Devil's Elbow, the Devil's Elbow bridge crosses the barrier with ease. The almost six-hundred-foot-long, two-span truss bridge was built in 1923 and carried cars high above the river. Although not remarkable from an engineering perspective, it is still a picturesque bridge and evokes memories of how travelers must have been looking forward to resting in Devil's Elbow. Today Interstate 44 crosses the Big Piney River a mere stone's throw from this bridge, and the cars zip by without a second look.

As we make our way farther down the Missouri portion of the highway, we come to Lebanon, which happens to have the famous Munger Moss Motel. Besides having a fabulous sign, The Munger Moss has been in continuous operation since the 1940s, and visiting it is a step back in time. Despite the pressures of being bypassed by the highway, it has continued as a Route 66 mainstay and likely will be for a long time to come.

Along Route 66 you will find signposts that give the mileage to various other points along the highway. Finding one is always a treat, and it is fun to see how far away various places are. Munger Moss is no different, except it has two excellent signposts.

Missouri   27

The Munger Moss also has a Motel sign still doing its best to lure passing travelers. This sign is tall and bright, and the red background against the blue sky makes an eye-catching contrast. Sometimes simple and to the point is best.

As we head down Route 66 just past Springfield, Interstate 44 diverges from Route 66. Up until now, the route of both is the same, as they mostly run parallel, sometimes crossing, sometimes not. Often Route 66 disappears, usually because of the interstate's placement on top of it. Sometimes Route 66 simply goes away for no discernible reason, and you have to take the interstate a while to catch up with it again. Now and then the two go their separate ways, as in this case. The results are dramatic. Route 66 will continue through Carthage, then Joplin, and through Kansas and into Oklahoma, while the interstate bypasses Kansas and heads directly into Oklahoma. To be fair, the interstate misses Kansas by six hundred feet, but still, it does. We will, of course, keep on Route 66.

As we head past Springfield and leave its bustle behind, we find ourselves on a deserted two-lane highway, and we are transported back in time. Few modern-day reminders exist now, and the straight road leads ever westward. We come to a stop sign seemingly there for no particular reason, and if we glance to the left, we'll see the remains of an old corner gas station. "Remains" in this case means two old gas pumps nestled in the weeds. The pumps read Keotane and Skeltane, an old Skelly brand of gas last sold in the 1970s. Legend has it that an entire gas station was here, which then faded away, but another story has it that these pumps were relocated here for about the same reason as the stop sign—no particular one. Either way, in the golden, fading afternoon light, the gas pumps offer a vivid reminder of yesterday.

Coming into the former town of Plano we find another stop sign randomly placed. Once the interstate opened, the entire village of Plano vanished, except for a few people who still live nearby. Plano, however, does contain a large, striking ruin that is the source of many rumors. The brick building built in a vaguely gothic style has no discernible markings and this has been said to be a mortuary (it wasn't), a casket company (it wasn't), or some other creepy building (it wasn't). According to a former mayor of Plano, it was a mercantile store in the early 1900s serving the surrounding area. The upper floor of the two-story structure hosted community events, some of which were mixers where the young men and women could get to know each other. It was the vibrant center and hub of Plano, and nothing untoward ever happened here.

Back on the highway and continuing west, we arrive at Gary's Gay Parita in Paris Springs. This old Sinclair station has a plethora of history. Built by Fred and Gay Mason in the 1930s, this station has long been a mainstay on the route. Primarily a Sinclair station, like so many others, it added a garage, allowing it to become a full-service station offering repairs and mechanical services. The garage, an unusual stone structure, instantly became iconic.

A fire swept through the station in the 1950s, leaving nothing worth salvaging. Normally such a fire would be the end of the business, but not the Gay Parita! In 2004 Gary Turner built a replica of the station to bring it back to life. Like magic, the legend was reborn, and the Mother Road had one of its icons back. Turner spent the rest of his days restoring and rebuilding the station, leaving behind a mostly completed work. Fate again conspired to take the icon away, and after Turner passed in 2015, the station began fading into yesterday.

Until Turner's daughter stepped in, that is. Barbara Turner and her husband moved from South Carolina to take over and restore the station for the second time. Proving that hard work and determination always makes the difference, today the Gay Parita is full of life and receiving visitors.

Next to the station is the stone garage where Fred worked miracles on cars and trucks. Sometimes he worked late into the night making repairs to get travelers back on the road. If you listen carefully, you can hear the radio playing in the background and the click-clack of his tools as he makes the final adjustments.

Finally it's time to leave Gay Parita. We drive into the deepening evening westward bound, as always. It has been a long day; it's time to think about where to spend the night. Carthage is just down the road, where we will seek lodging.

Spencer, Missouri, is a small time capsule. Situated along an ancient segment of Route 66, Spencer quickly faded away when a more efficient alignment bypassed it. Spencer is being restored, however, and today the tidy row of rock buildings looks as it used to. Spencer contains a Phillips 66 station, a café, and a few other empty storefronts, but its days of selling gasoline and serving good food are long over.

Perhaps the café will reopen as Spencer comes back to life.

This view is looking eastward from Spencer as the sun is beginning to set. The original Portland Concrete recedes into the distance and over a small steel truss pony bridge. The view is exactly the way it was in the 1930s, giving another pristine glimpse into the past.

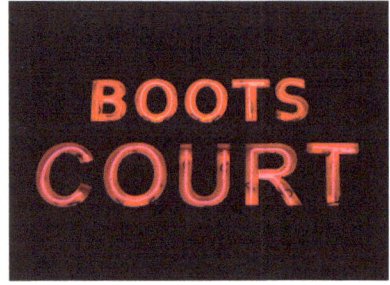 

By the time we arrive in Carthage, night has fallen, and it is time to look for a motel. The bright neon lights of Boots Court pierce the night, letting us know that our search is over. It is hard to miss Boots Court at night. Not only is the bright Boots Court neon sign glowing, but also the entire motel is bathed in green neon, truly a beacon to travelers.

Arriving at the motel, we are relieved to see the lit vacancy sign. Whew! Now we know where we'll be spending the night, and there is no better place than Boots Court.

Boots Court is a motor lodge, even to this day. You can park your car in a carport, or if you are lucky a garage, right next to your comfortable room. Upon opening the door to your room, you will find the radio in the corner playing softly, the lights welcoming you, and the comfortable bed waiting for you.

Boots Court was built in 1949 and remains perfectly frozen in time. You won't find any fancy LED clocks by the side of the bed, but you will find a wind-up clock there. The bells on top do an excellent job of waking you in the morning and are a refreshing change from the harsh "buzz-beep" of today's wailing alarms. There are no modern televisions in the rooms, or for that matter, any televisions at all, since TV didn't come to Carthage until the early 1950s. What you will find is a comfortable room and a relaxing experience, no matter what year the outside world believes it is.

Leaving Carthage we pass by the historic 66 Drive-In, which is the place to be on weekends. The 66 Drive-In also opened in 1949, and like Boots Court remains frozen in time, although to be fair, it does play modern-day movies. In today's world of modern multi-screen indoor cineplexes, it is marvelous to see a drive-in theater still thriving, and people still coming out to sit in their cars and watch movies on the weekend.

Before we know it, the Missouri state line appears, and we find ourselves in Kansas.

Kansas

Route 66 slices through the southeastern corner of Kansas for only thirteen miles, making it by far the shortest segment of the states it traverses. Even though Kansas claims only a few miles of the famous route, there is quite a lot of Route 66 to visit, yesterday or today.

Pulling into Galena, the first city on Route 66 in Kansas, we find this Kanotex sign. Kanotex was based in Arkansas City, Kansas, so it is fitting that the first sign we encounter is from a Kansas company. Kanotex was a regional company and never spread very far away from its home state until Anderson-Prichard Oil Corporation acquired it in the early 1950s. Today the Kanotex station has been restored as a curio shop and diner.

You can't get any more apropos for Kansas than an old trailer for Western Kansas Express. It's been a while since this trailer was on the road, but it rests quietly alongside the highway, perhaps hoping it will be loaded with cargo. It will be waiting a very long time.

A trendy space for advertising was the side of buildings, especially brick buildings. Today we don't see this technique used often, which is a shame, because it is part advertising and part artwork. In Galena, we find an excellent example for Pepsi and Mountain Dew on the former Buck's Recreation building.

These two masterpieces, spanning the width of the building, are slowly fading away, which just adds to their charm. When the signs were first painted, Buck's was a thriving bar. That's no longer the case, and the signage is succumbing to the relentless sun. Still, they are here for us to enjoy, for now.

A block away from Buck's we find this Texaco sign reminding us that we can fill up before continuing our journey out of Galena. The pumps are long gone, and the building it is next to has certainly seen better days, but the sign itself continues to stand bright and tall.

Leo Williams opened Williams' Store in Riverton in 1925, and it has remained open and in the same location ever since. Serving Riverton as well Route 66 travelers, this store has been a mainstay of the small community. In the 1930s and 1940s, official route guides and maps included it, which cemented its place in history.

In 1973 the market was sold to Joe Eisler. It has been in the family ever since, now operating by his nephew as Nelson's Old Riverton Store. The store has remained mostly unchanged since the beginning, allowing us to experience early life on Route 66.

Baxter Springs is the third and final city on this short segment in Kansas, and it too is rich in Route 66 history. In the middle of Baxter Springs is the current day visitor center, which was at first Independent Oil and Gas and later a Phillips 66 station. This station is another excellent example of the cottage-style filling station. Like its brethren in Illinois, it was neighborhood-based and tried to evoke an air of "home." Like so many others, it slowly expanded over the years by adding repair facilities. It was a mainstay of Baxter Springs and continues to provide services, albeit a different kind, on Route 66.

If you look down at the driveway area, you'll see a Kansas Route 66 sign painted on the concrete. Placing the route shields on the roadway itself was a common way of marking routes, and all across the country you can still find painted highway shield signs often faded almost beyond recognition. This practice is coming back into fashion, although for different reasons. Route 66 signs are attractive targets for thieves, but they have a much harder time taking shields painted on highways.

After a mere 12.8 official miles, we leave Kansas and head into Oklahoma.

Oklahoma

Oklahoma marks a transition in our journey. We've been traveling more or less in a southwest direction, but now we head due west, making a beeline to California. We also transition from the gently rolling hills and green countryside to the classic western landscape. We enter Oklahoma amid lush trees, and we leave it dodging tumbleweeds. All along the way, Route 66 looms large.

Just inside of Oklahoma we encounter an excellent example of brick art in Quapaw. Some brick murals are advertisements, and others depict scenes, but this display represents businesses. Like many of these murals, this one is slowly fading and being overtaken by weeds. Eventually this piece of Americana will be only a memory.

This 1931 Marathon station in Commerce is now repurposed as a Dairy King. By all accounts, the gas station did well and was a popular stop along Route 66, but in the late 1950s and early 1960s, new highways were built, like Interstate 44. The interstate bypassed Commerce, causing the station to close. This situation is a common theme along the stretch of Route 66 from the Oklahoma state line to Tulsa, and almost every business, including the towns themselves, struggled to survive. Not everyone was able to overcome the loss of traffic, and many places have gone by the wayside. In any event, this building was spared and even partially restored to resemble the former station. Right across the street from the Dairy King is the 1929 Hole in the Wall Conoco Station. This small filling station seems to jut out of a brick wall, and when you step back and look at it, it just shouldn't be there. The station was reportedly a Phillips 66 although it now sports a Conoco sign.

There are a few examples of the cottage-style Conoco station along Route 66, but this is the best example. Although it is broken down and run down, the lights in the gas pumps are still lit. Like its neighbor, this station could not hold on.

This old Coca-Cola sign hangs next to the Hole in the Wall gas station. As much as it is resisting the elements, it too is losing its battle.

All along the length of Route 66 you'll find a few restaurants that everyone seems to know, such as Ted Drewes and the Cozy Dog. Waylan's Ku-Ku, in Miami, never quite achieved nationwide fame, but it is well known in the surrounding area. Its sign sports a different shade of green than most, making it stand out. In the early 1960s, there were quite a few Ku-Kus, especially in the Midwest, but over time, most of them vanished for various reasons. This particular one, however, continues to hold on and is still a stop for those cruising Route 66.

Years ago if you needed a place to spend the night in Afton, you might have considered the Rest Haven Motel. Unfortunately this motel saw its last guest check out quite some time ago. Afton was once a popular destination and was known for the Buffalo Ranch. The "ranch" featured a few larger animals such as the namesake buffalo, as well as llamas. The Buffalo Ranch has long since been torn down and replaced by the modern-day Buffalo Ranch Travel Center. Afton isn't as popular as it once was, and many businesses, such as the Rest Haven, are only memories.

Oklahoma   41

If you happen to be driving your Packard through Afton and you develop car trouble, you're in luck. An approved Packard Service station happens to be here that is more than capable of attending to your needs. Although that story sounds good in theory, the mechanics have moved on, and getting service will not be possible. Maybe you're not in luck after all.

In actuality, the Packard sign is part of Afton Station, a 1930s DX station, which is now a visitor's center. Although you can no longer have your Packard serviced, you can browse the collection of Packards here. The station also has beautifully restored DX pumps out front.

Best of all, we encounter another utterly fantastic mileage sign. This sign leans casually on the station and lets us know that we have 1,680 more miles until we reach our destination at Santa Monica, California. Note too the blue whale next to Tulsa. We'll stop there.

We continue westward down the highway.

Just outside Afton rests Avon Court. Built in the 1930s and operating through 1958, this auto court has been completely abandoned. It's incredible how these relics survive in any form at all until the modern day. Originally the Avon Court consisted of seven units, each with a carport, although today only three units remain. Needless to say, they are not in good shape.

One of the hallmarks of the old highway system was that the highways followed the contours of the land and for a large part blended in. Today's interstates plow straight through the landscape. The Pryor Creek Bridge near Chelsea is an excellent example of the highway being harmonious with the land.

This small single-truss bridge, built in 1926, carried Route 66 traffic until 1932. The bridge is 123 feet long and just nineteen feet wide, allowing it to be relatively unobtrusive, at least for a bridge. In 1932 a new alignment went just north of this bridge, and the bridge segment fell into disuse.

The disused segment, however, also brings home another point: motoring, especially in the early days of the Mother Road, was an enjoyable experience. The narrow, slower-speed roads were staggeringly scenic. Imagine crossing this bridge as it arcs over the river, passing through and under tall trees shading your way. Crossing this bridge today is a pleasant experience, and you can reminisce how the motoring experience must have been. Of course today it is all about efficiency, and a bridge like this will never carry significant traffic again.

Coming into Chelsea we find the sign for its namesake motel. Although the sign remains, the destroyed neon tubes mean the sign won't light. As for the 1930s-era motel itself, it is private property and a shell of its former self. Although it is a shame to see signs and buildings such as these slide into obscurity, it is also nice to see that something remains. Perhaps one day it will be restored and relit, like many others have been. We cross our fingers and hope.

We continue down the highway, and just before we reach Tulsa, we come to the iconic Blue Whale swimming hole in Catoosa. Built in 1972, the Blue Whale is a relative latecomer to the Mother Road, but it quickly became a favorite, and often appears on signposts across the country. Built by Hugh Davis, the Blue Whale has long been a popular swimming place, although it has closed down, undergone refurbishment, and changed hands, all of which is not uncommon for buildings and businesses on Route 66.

In any event, the Blue Whale is a must-do destination and has invited travelers to stop, take a dip, and cool off. The whale itself is hollow, and you can walk through the mouth to the end and jump off into the lake or use one of the slides. On a hot summer day, the squeals of the children and adults are a delight to hear.

The Rose Bowl in Tulsa has endured a difficult history. Built in 1962, it once, much like its brethren in other cities, flourished as bowling swept America in the 1960s. Like others, business began a long, slow decline, and the Rose Bowl eventually shut its doors. Normally that would be the end of the story, but not so with the Rose Bowl. For whatever reason, it was subject to not one but two arson attempts. The building itself was gutted, but the exterior remained unscathed. In 2006 it was sold to a local businessman, but a non-compete agreement with AMF prevents it from reopening as a bowling alley.

Today the Rose Bowl is an event center and open sporadically. Although not quite the same, at least this architecturally unusual building remains standing on Route 66.

As Route 66 wends its way through Tulsa, a few icons remain scattered here and there. Some tucked away locations are easy to overlook. Others, like the Meadow Gold sign, are big, bold, and impossible to miss.

From the 1930s until the 1970s the Meadow Gold sign stood tall at the corner of 11th and Lewis, a beacon in the night for all those years. Meadow Gold was a milk company serving Tulsa, and business was strong, at least for a few decades. Alas, in the 1970s the owner of the building the sign was on decided to raze the building, which was horrible news for the sign. It was taken down, and Tulsa and Route 66 lost one of the larger and more memorable signs. Such an event would normally mean the end of the sign, but not this time. A new purpose-built pavilion for the sign was constructed at 11th and Quaker, two blocks away from the original location. The sign itself was restored and placed atop its new home. The sign remains, preserved and protected, once again a beacon on Route 66.

We'll leave Tulsa behind and head for Oklahoma City to see what treasures we can find there.

Our first stop outside of Tulsa is in Sapulpa. We've talked about bowling on Route 66 already, but by no means was bowling the only entertainment. Rollerskating was another popular activity, then and now, although less common now. Fortunately the Route 66 Roller Dome is there to help us out. Following a familiar theme, this rink opened in the heyday of Route 66, the early 1950s, and then closed once the interstate subsumed Route 66. It was brought back to life as a church and then once again as a skating rink. Although it is sad when a business closes, it is a joyous occasion when it comes back to us. Skate on!

Sapulpa also has a beautiful example of an advertising brick mural, this one extolling the virtues of Mentholatum, an ointment for headaches, muscle pain, red or dry eyes, constipation, colds, chapped lips, and a host of other ailments, which is still commercially available. This topical ointment, it seems, will cure just about anything you have. The copyright date of this mural is 1918, although it probably has been restored. It is an excellent example of how powerful these murals can be.

We've talked about the open road and mentioned the original Portland Concrete surface. Now is another opportunity to see how it looks. Just outside of Bristow we find a few miles of original Route 66. The lanes are quite a bit smaller than roadways built later. Besides being made entirely of concrete, there is no shoulder at all, ever, and when the road is flat, like here, there aren't even any curbs or gutters. The road has gentle sloping curbs added when it goes up or downhill, but only on the parts of the road that rise or fall. This segment gives us an excellent example of what it was like to travel the road, moving endlessly forever forward, gently following the counters of the land, and blending into the landscape. No wonder Route 66 has captured our hearts and our minds!

In the later years many, if not most, of the surviving segments were paved over with blacktop, so finding a pristine section is rare and exciting. To find a portion that is drivable is even more exciting, and to find one in fantastic shape as this one makes it amazing. This segment will not be the last such segment we visit, though.

Today Stroud, Oklahoma, genuinely embraces Route 66, just as it has for all these years. The main drag is just a few blocks long, but those few blocks have three excellent sites. One of the first iconic signs we encounter is for the Rock Café. The Rock Café has been in business since the late 1930s, usually as a café, although it operated as a Greyhound bus terminal for a while before reverting to a café. In later years, a fire ravaged it, forcing it to close briefly before opening again. Resiliency is another common theme on Route 66.

Just a half block away from the Rock Café is this beautiful brick mural in remarkably good condition. These murals are a joy to find, and every one makes you stop and spend some time looking at it.

Continuing west a couple of blocks, we come to the Skyliner Motel. This sign is an excellent example from the late 1950s and early 1960s. The pylon design has a large compressed arrow and stacked lettering and was common along Route 66. What makes this sign interesting is that it is simple and visually striking. It still calls visitors in for a night's rest, so it must be part of the Skyliner's continued success.

This ever-classic 66 Bowl sign in Chandler has been relocated from Oklahoma City. The sign's entire life has been spent on Route 66, albeit in two different places. The original 66 Bowl opened in 1959. These days the sign once again advertises bowling lanes.

Right on the main street in Chandler we find this restored Phillips 66 sign. Another small cottage station stood here that long ago saw its last customer. It is nice to see so many restored signs along the Mother Road.

Sometimes a structure is so old that no one remembers anything about it. People still want to know its history, and thus a legend or a myth is born. Why let a few facts stand in the way of a good story? With a lead in like that one, you know you're going to hear just such a story.

Partway between Luther and Arcadia, you can find this small stone structure. Given its location and shape, it was an early gas station, probably from the late 1910s or early 1920s. The two pillars in front would have supported the canopy. There is no sign of a garage or repair bays, which stations typically built later, so we can reasonably surmise that it went out of business before those added services became popular, sometime around 1940, give or take a few years. Scant records exist for this building, so forward we venture into supposition.

The owners of the Rock of Ages Farm, who own the land this structure sits on, placed a small weathered sign that tells us that this building was indeed a gas station, had two pumps, and didn't have electricity, all of which is reasonably supported by what we see. The sign goes on to tell us that the station sold cold soda on days when the ice man came through, which again tracks with what we would guess. So far, so good.

The sign then goes on to say that times were hard, and making ends meet was difficult. Somehow or other, the owner of this station joined forces with a "so-called salesman" who had printing plates for ten-dollar bills. After adding a small room to the back, the station sold gas out front and produced counterfeit ten-dollar bills out back. Whether any of this information is true is anyone's guess. It does, after all, sound like quite the tall tale. Walking around out back reveals no remains of a back room, which could mean that it is entirely gone like the rest of the station, or that it was never there. Others tell the story that yes, there was a counterfeiting ring here, but it passed the bills to a hidden room in the back, with nary a mention of actually making money there. As to be expected, others say that the story is all complete hogwash and nothing like that happened.

We will probably never know the truth of the story. But you just never know.

Route 66 next heads into Oklahoma City, where for all practical purposes it turns and now travels due west. We continue toward Santa Monica.

Before we arrive in California, we have to make a few more stops along the way, the first being Owl Court in Oklahoma City. The Owl Court, built in the 1930s, is on an early alignment of Route 66. At one time the motor court included a gas station and a café, making it an ideal destination. It fared well, but not well enough, and eventually fell into disuse. People have talked about renovation plans, but so far no one has brought this location back to its glory years.

A Coca-Cola sign at one time hung on the side of the building, alongside an unusual owl ideogram. This faded, weathered and time-worn sign survived through the descent of the Owl Court, persevering until someone stole it in 2017. Bad enough that Route 66 icons suffer the ignominy of fading away, but to have parts of them stolen is beyond comprehension.

Motel Ranger in El Reno is a typical Route 66 motel. Low and sleek, it occupies a high-traffic location, which has allowed it to survive. Although its sign is not neon, it is still a classic sign, especially at night.

The Centre Theater in El Reno began showing movies in 1944, and like all theaters at that time, was a focal point for the town. Like many other buildings, it eventually wound down and ran down, falling into disrepair. Even the facade crashed down to the sidewalk. The theater has been fully restored, including its stunning marquee, and now hosts occasional events.

We're through Oklahoma City and its surrounding smaller cities. Once again the road opens up, although this time with a different character. We left behind the rolling green hills at the Kansas state line and began seeing only rolling hills. Now we're leaving the rolling hills, and the land flattens out for a long way.

Heading west we leave behind the cottage-style stations. That isn't to say that you can't find them in the west, but they become uncommon. In this part of Oklahoma, a different style station, the "over the drive" design, was far more widespread. Carl Ditmore built the Provine Station in 1929 and then managed it for five years. In 1934 W. O. Waldrop purchased the station and named it the Provine Station. It stayed that way until 1941, when Lucille and Carl Hamons became the new owners. The Hamons ran the station for fifty-nine years—an impressive feat.

The preserved station remains a landmark on Route 66 for generations of travelers to experience.

When we cruise through the town of Clinton we encounter an authentic Valentine Diner. We have to point out the word authentic because a little while later we'll encounter a diner that looks like a Valentine, but isn't.

This diner was originally located in Shamrock, Texas, and was known as the Porter House Café. Like most if not all the Valentines on Route 66, business dried up, and it was forced to close. Some of these diners have found new purposes, such as the one that became a police substation in Albuquerque, New Mexico. This particular Valentine Diner was spared, moved to Clinton, and fully restored as a typical diner.

What is so special about a Valentine Diner? The Valentine Diner Company manufactured these compact and efficient units in Wichita, Kansas. The diners had eight to ten stools and were relatively inexpensive to acquire, typically five thousand dollars. Prospective owners would order a diner, and it would arrive on a railcar. From there owners would add whatever personal touches they wished, name their business as they desired, and open their doors to customers. It was like a diner business in a box. One interesting feature of the business model was the repayment plan. The owner deposited a percentage of each day's take in a dedicated lockbox that came with every diner. A company representative regularly came around, often catching a ride on the railroads, and emptied the lockbox.

Valentine offered several models of its diner, and in later years, some were able to seat up to sixty-four customers. Our diner is most likely the "Master" model, a ten-stool version of the design made in the early 1950s.

Perhaps we can find someone to whip us up a burger and fries, a popular order at a Valentine Diner.

Considering the amount of progress made over the years and how many buildings have been replaced, modernized, or demolished, it is tough for us to peer back in time. Sayer, however, provides one of those rare opportunities. The downtown historic district, looking toward the courthouse, appears almost exactly as it did back in the heyday of Route 66. The only alteration to this photograph was the removal of a modern communications tower, a modern yellow traffic sign, and a yield sign.

This view also features the Stovall Theater. Opened in 1950, the Stovall was the centerpiece of the town. It was also the only entertainment for miles around, which guaranteed it business, at least until the interstate bypassed Sayre and Sayer began declining. The theater, long closed, was in desperate need of demolition or repairs when cooler heads made the latter choice, and today, thanks to extensive renovation, the theater appears as it did in the 1950s.

We point our wheels west; the Texas state line is up ahead.

Texas

Route 66 cuts across the Texas panhandle in a straight line. Along it we transition to more of the Wild West. In between the small towns lie long stretches of empty, lonely highway punctuated only by tumbleweed and blowing dust. Texas is rich in Route 66 history and lore, despite its short amount of highway.

We begin our headlong plunge straight across Texas, and we can't help marveling that we are driving under large, open skies. We can see for miles to either side and yet not see anything. The unbroken ribbon of concrete and pavement ahead calls us ever forward, and forward we drive. Our first stop is Shamrock and the large Conoco station there. We've been able to see it for a while, especially at night, since it has tall neon-lit towers thrusting into the sky. It promises a welcome oasis.

Originally built in 1936, this complex has gas, repair facilities, and a café, making it the perfect place to stop. It is of an unusual design featuring twin towers, which is unique to the entire length of Route 66. The towers gave it its name of Tower Service Station. It featured neon lighting throughout the station, art deco details, and glazed ceramic tiles. This station saw a tremendous amount of business and was the place to stop. The U-Drop Inn Cafe, in the same complex, became known for "delicious food courteously served." The third building, originally designated as retail space, instead quickly became overflow seating because of the popularity of the café.

When the interstate passed north of the once busy intersection traffic no longer flowed by the station, and Tower Station began its long decline. In the 1970s, it became a FINA station, complete with FINA's blue and white livery, where it continued until the 1990s.

The station has been fully restored, including its iconic glazed tiles, and once again it appears much as it did in the early days. Just like yesterday, you can see the glow of the towers at night for miles, and just like yesterday, you feel a sense of awe as you drive up to it. In a lovely call to the past, the nearby modern-day Conoco station also sports the same overall design and neon lighting and matches Tower Station. While you fill your gas tank, you can't help feeling what it was like to do the same back in the day.

A little way down the road from Shamrock we come to the town of McLean and its rattlesnakes. Route 66 was far more than just gas stations and motels. It also had attractions. For many, Route 66 was as much about the journey as the destination, and for those, stopping at the various attractions was a must-do. High on the list of attractions were snakes, and the most popular of all snakes were rattlesnakes. Rattlesnake museums become something of a cottage industry in the western portion of the road. All are long gone, and most of the buildings that housed them are gone, too. McLean has a lonely sign letting us know we could have stopped and enjoyed one of our first opportunities to see live rattlesnakes.

McLean also has a somewhat restored Phillips 66 gas station and Phillips truck. This cottage-style station, the last we'll see on our trek west, is done in the old Phillips 66 orange. The truck next to it is a nice touch as well. The station, built in roughly 1929, is the first Phillips 66 station anywhere in Texas, and since it still with us today, also has the distinction of being the oldest Phillips 66 in Texas as well. This beautiful example of an early Phillips 66 sign hangs at the station. All that is missing from this small station is gasoline. The restoration took a couple of shortcuts, such as painting windows instead of making windows. Still, we get the idea of how it looked.

Texas

Heading west through the small town of Alanreed, we might be able to catch a glimpse of this old Texaco station. This filling station is unusual in that it has two canopies, facing in opposite directions. This arrangement allowed drivers to fill up no matter their current direction, an excellent, and in inclement weather welcome, convenience. Despite its dual canopies, it was not able to survive.

Because Route 66 was such a busy route, businesses in the more isolated stretches didn't have to advertise much or even at all to attract customers. Sometimes, though, one had to work at it a bit harder. One way businesses enticed potential customers was by constructing something eye-catching. The curious traveler would stop in, and owners hoped they would end up making a purchase or two. Most businesses used a sign of some sort, and many used neon signs. Some used giant signs or even billboards, and then there was the truck stop at Britten, which took things in a whole different direction.

Ralph Britten had a truck stop just outside of Groom that did well enough, but it could do better. Ralph managed to purchase a water tower in the early 1980s. He placed it next to his truck stop, but to make it more enticing for Route 66 travelers, he built it leaning at an angle. The tower looks like it will fall over at any moment and is barely holding on. Naturally travelers stopped to see if it was going to fall. Just as naturally, they ended up in the truck stop. The leaning tower of Britten was and still is marketing at its very best.

The truck stop burned down some years ago, and the water tower still hasn't managed to fall over. Yet.

Route 66 has a little bit of everything.

As we come into Vega we find the first Magnolia Gas Station of our journey. Built by J. T. Owen in 1924, before Route 66 existed in Vega, it served travelers on the Ozark Trail. Route 66 came through Vega and was routed by this station, even though the road went out of its way to do so. Vega is an excellent example of the road not going straight, but rather taking a circuitous route. What is even more interesting is that east of town, Route 66 turns north and begins its city tour, but from where it turns north, you can see where it ends its winding route through Vega, just a couple of blocks away. Eventually the highway department made the route straight, just as it should have been in the first place.

The Magnolia station did an excellent business and became one of the go-to stops on the road, at least until 1937, when Route 66 was rerouted straight through Vega. Even then, the station managed to hang on until the early 1950s. It served as a barbershop and then closed. Restored and preserved, the station found new life as a visitor center. The arrows, added behind the station in 2014, had nothing to do with the station itself; however, they sure do look neat, and the next giant arrows we come across will be part of Route 66.

According to the Texas Historical Association, Magnolia Gas was formed in 1911 from several other companies, a common practice in the petroleum industry. Magnolia performed well and continued to grow. In 1931 Magnolia began using the red Pegasus logo that we see here and there on the road. In 1959 it began doing business as Mobil Oil and Gas, a name we see today as the ExxonMobile company. We might not recognize the name Magnolia, but we certainly see its logo.

Adrian is an exciting stop for us because we reach the halfway point of our journey, but just before it is the Bent Door Station. The Bent Door Station, built in the late 1940s, was a Phillip 66 mainstay on the road. The Bent Door claims it is the midpoint of Route 66, at least according to the crude signpost. The Bent Door began its decline and slowly dwindled away when the interstate bypassed Adrian. The Bent Door sat for many years until purchased with the intent of being restored and rehabilitated into a 1950s-style diner. The plans did not work out, though, and the Bent Door remains a relic of the Mother Road.

Whew! All of that history made us work up an appetite. Luckily there just happens to be a café here. Let's eat!

The MidPoint Cafe was built in the late 1940s and has served travelers on Route 66 since then. In its heyday, before Adrian was bypassed by Interstate 40, the café was open twenty-four hours a day. Originally known as Zella's, it has undergone owner changes and name changes several times and also suffered from a fire that resulted in rebuilding. In 1992 the name MidPoint Cafe was given to the building to capitalize on the fact that it probably is on the midpoint of Route 66. Again, marketing at its best. The MidPoint Cafe looks poised to continue its tradition. Let's hope that it does.

With lunch over, we can now pay some proper attention to the whole "midpoint" issue.

According to the Texas Highway of Transportation, this is the exact midpoint of Route 66, and thus the halfway marker of our journey. The sign is located a stone's throw from the Bent Door and the MidPoint Cafe, so surely one of these three places is indeed the midpoint. Given the numerous reroutings, alignments, and changes of Route 66, it is impossible to mark with any degree of confidence the exact midpoint. If this is it or not depends entirely on the year, and even the day of the year you are using for the calculation.

Since we need a halfway point, we'll use this one. It is 1,139 miles to Chicago and 1,139 miles to Santa Monica, or something like that.

This point, too, is a demarcation in our journey. So far we've encountered quite a few surviving businesses and fully restored icons on the Mother Road. Here and there, of course, we came across structures long abandoned, but generally we could see what it looked like "back in the day." As we continue west, however, this is not the case.

For whatever reason, from here on out not as many fully restored places exist for us to visit. There are some, and some of the places, as you will see, are fascinating. In general, though, we will now visit more abandoned places and see them how they are today, or least how they are before they completely fade away.

Maybe this decay is a result of land availability. In many of the western locations it is easier to let a building stand as it is and let the elements do the rest, while you rebuild next to or near the original structure. In the East, developers are more likely to tear down a structure and build where the original stood. Perhaps buildings in the West aren't as often repaired for some other reason entirely. In any event, we are at a turning point, so our view will change.

We motor on westward and straight into New Mexico.

New Mexico

Route 66 crosses the central part of New Mexico, making its way from the Texas border to the Arizona border. Here we encounter more of the Wild West, and the history and culture of the Mother Road is alive and well. True, we have as much of a chance of encountering a tumbleweed as a person, but the people we do meet are interesting characters.

New Mexico and Route 66 have a fascinating relationship. The road has always entered from Texas and left by way of Arizona, but it hasn't always been in a straight line. For a while it was anything but straight across the state. The original Mother Road went northeast to Santa Fe and then straight south, passing through Albuquerque to Los Lunas, where it turned again and headed northwest for a while before heading due west to Arizona. The route made no sense at all when you looked at a map, but at that time, the route was more about connecting local roads instead of being part of a national highway system.

In 1937 the Federal Highway System realigned Route 66 to be a straight line across the state, reducing it to from 507 miles to just 399. Quite a difference! Stories abound about this alignment, should you choose to believe them. They involve intentionally routing the road straight across the state to avoid Santa Fe as part of political payback. While that theory may well be the case, merely looking at the map says that the post-1937 alignment makes the most sense.

Although we don't often talk about alignments, in this case, we need to. We'll be following only the post-1937 alignment. Although the original alignment had some of the best, and worst, roads the state of New Mexico had to offer, virtually all of it has disappeared. New Mexico's transportation department, for better or worse, has a policy of reusing what it can, so the original roadbed was consumed by other, modern-day highways. The businesses along the route in Santa Fe and Los Lunas are long gone and the original concrete pavement long removed. Mere echoes of the past are along this alignment, so we'll leave those shadows for another day.

The same policy of reuse means that much of the original roadway in New Mexico has been repurposed, usually by Interstate 40. Very few pieces of original concrete remain. Also in short supply are the original businesses that once supported and in turn were supported by Route 66. As we will see, though, not all are departed, and the ones that remain are arguably as busy as they were "back in the day."

New Mexico saw some of the last "official" Route 66 traffic, which continued up until 1985, when Route 66 was officially decertified. It took twenty-five years to build Interstate 40 through New Mexico, and thanks to "staged construction," where road crews made a portion at a time, the larger cities continued to receive Route 66 traffic. Eventually the interstate was the only efficient way, if not the only way, to move east to west across New Mexico. As a side note and a nod to the best-laid plans, in the late 1940s and 1950s, cities such as Tucumcari, Gallup, and Grants upgraded Route 66 through their boundaries in anticipation of the Federal Aid Highway Act of 1956 and the new highway system that it would bring. Their thought was that the new highway would flow through their towns, and they wanted to be ready for it. Each of these cities spent the time, effort, and precious funds to improve the roadway, widening it, where possible, to four lines. They were ready and intended to be leaders when the new highway opened. Instead they were all stunned when the interstate bypassed them, causing the same issues as in every other state.

Only a few strips of the original Route 66 remain in New Mexico, mostly as a frontage road for the interstate. We'll stop chatting about the highway for the rest of New Mexico and instead focus on the cities and sites.

With that information, we head into New Mexico.

We don't get very far before we make our first stop at Glen Rio. Glen Rio straddles the state line, which made for a few unusual situations. For example, no bars existed on the Texas side because Deaf Smith County was dry. Conversely, there were no gasoline stations on the New Mexico side because New Mexico taxes were higher than those in Texas. Talk about taking advantage of your situation! In any event, Glen Rio was a thriving community, with Route 66 providing one hundred percent of its economy.

This small diner looks a lot like a Valentine Diner, except it's not. It is a knockoff. The Brownlee Diner, later known as the Little Juárez Diner, was constructed out of cinderblocks to look exactly like a Valentine Diner. After all, why mess with a perfectly good design? The cinderblocks give it away, though, since authentic Valentine Diners were not, in fact, made of cinderblocks.

Like the rest of Glen Rio, this diner declined rapidly when the interstate bypassed Glen Rio in the 1970s, and Glen Rio itself quickly deteriorated to a shell of what it was.

Once we leave the faded lights of Glen Rio behind, our next stop is Tucumcari. Tucumcari has always aggressively advertised itself with the slogan "Tucumcari Tonight!" Let's go see what the fuss is all about.

We've talked about the various types of businesses along the Mother Road, including gas stations, motels, blue whales, and rattlesnakes. As we head into the far western states, we pick up another favorite spot for the traveler: the trading post, or as we like to refer to them in today's terms, a souvenir shop. With a stone teepee, or wigwam, out front to further reinforce the idea that you will be "trading," the TePee offers everything travelers might ever want to purchase as a memento of their Route 66 trip. The only thing being "traded" was American dollars for some souvenir or other, but that is beside the point. Trading Posts are part of the tapestry of Route 66, and far too many of them have closed. It is nice to see this one still going strong.

Across the street from TePee Curios is the iconic Blue Swallow Motel, thriving along the highway.

Built in 1939, the Blue Swallow was open for business in 1940 with ten rooms and offered convenient garages for your car. An attractive motor court, its pink stucco walls have embedded-shell motifs. It was an unusual combination, the shells and stucco, but it works and adds to the charm. As to be expected, the Blue Swallow made extensive use of neon lights.

Tucumcari and all its businesses suffered when the interstate bypassed the city, despite plans to future-proof it. The Blue Swallow was no exception, but it hung on, although it was in dire need of repairs. Eventually new owners purchased it, renovated it, and kept it alive.

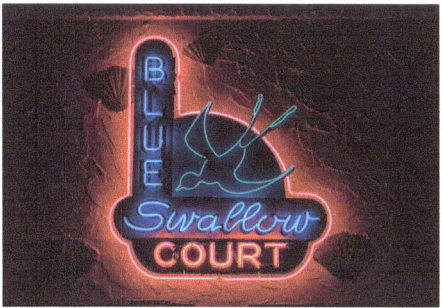

The Blue Swallow also features a throwback to the early days of traveling by the use of its colorful chairs. In those days, meaning in the days before television was in every motel room, the concept of checking in and then settling in to watch TV didn't exist. Instead guests socialized outside their rooms, relaxing in the chairs. In that tradition, the entire property has a large and colorful selection of chairs for you, just like Funks Grove in Illinois.

The Blue Swallow is one of the more popular destinations on the whole highway and is known from end to end.

Across the street from the Blue Swallow is Motel Safari with its apt sign. You don't see a lot of people on camels around New Mexico, or anywhere in the Southwest for that matter, which makes Motel Safari a must-stop location on our journey. If you look closely, below the sign you can see the Blue Swallow and a Pontiac parked there. Perhaps someone is checking in?

New Mexico 67

For our final stop in Tucumcari, we'll continue to Tucumcari's far western edge and the site of the former Paradise Motel. Not long ago the Paradise was open for business, but like many other businesses, could no longer make a go of it once the interstate bypassed Tucumcari. The sign, however, has a bit more history to it.

The sign had fallen into a similar state of disrepair as the motel, meaning it was pretty far gone; however, in 2003 it was restored. During the restoration project, workers discovered that the sign had been altered, possibly because of a previous restoration somewhere along the line, leaving a bit of a puzzle as to how, exactly, the final restored sign should appear. In the end, a decision was made to restore the top half as it always was, while the lower half was partly new work. Originally the Paradise had a pool, but that had been filled in. Having a person diving into a nonexistent pool didn't make much sense, so the restoration team made the figure dive into the word "open" which made, well, not much more sense, but it was making the best of the situation. Sadly the sign is no longer lit and needs another restoration. Sometimes a sign has more history than the property it touts, especially when it comes to neons.

As we roll into Santa Rosa, it's probably time to fill up the old gas tank again. We wheel up to the Rio Pecos Ranch Truck Stop and realize that we're a little too late, as in a couple of decades, since it closed its doors long ago. Opening in the mid-1950s or perhaps the early 1960s, the Rio Pecos served the semis of the road and saw quite a bit of traffic. Suffering the same decline as so many others, it closed in the 1980s, leaving only the signage and the repair garage standing. There are plans to one day redevelop the property, and we can only hope that it happens before anything else is torn down.

This remarkable café sign still attracts travelers today. With its still-bright colors and classic white-and-red motif, it draws attention when the sky is pure blue. Directly under the sign is the Santa Rose Grill, which has survived the downturn in traffic and remains a staple on the route.

If the year were 1959, which it isn't, we could stay at the newly opened Sunset Motel in Moriarty. Although it isn't 1959 anymore, we can still stay at the motel, and even better, at night its neon sign still lights up for us. Located east of Albuquerque, this motel is perfect for the traveler not quite able or willing to push on to Albuquerque. Moriarty is a relative latecomer to Route 66 in New Mexico, but it made a lasting impression. Originally Route 66 looped northward through Santa Fe and then back southward through Albuquerque, missing the towns to the east of Albuquerque. When the new, straighter alignment came through, however, towns such as Moriarty found themselves on the Mother Road, allowing motels such as the Sunset Motel to rise and flourish.

Down the street from the Sunset Motel we find a still-open Whiting Brothers service station, although today it is a small tire shop.

The Whiting Brothers stations play a part of the story of the Mother Road. Like Shell and Standard Oil, Whiting Brothers was an early gasoline supplier in the Southwest. Starting in 1926, the Whiting Brothers built relatively inexpensive stations using local lumber and materials and often located filling stations on the edges of towns. They took full advantage of Route 66 and built up and down the route from Texas through California, as well as elsewhere in those states. Their distinctive architecture let motorists know what was coming up, and with the promise of cheap gasoline, the stations did quite well. As the years went on, the Whiting Brothers expanded into motels, cafés, and even souvenir shops, which further extended their empire.

Despite the company's infrastructure, however, Whiting Brothers gradually wound down operations in the 1980s, either selling or abandoning the stations. A few have survived and been repurposed into other businesses, and a couple still operate under a different name. This one in Moriarty continues operation, although it no longer sells gasoline. At least it gives us the best, and only, example of a pristine Whiting Brothers sign.

From Moriarty, Route 66 heads toward Albuquerque, a major city on the route. It crosses the high desert into the Sandia Mountains, where it descends through Tijeras Canyon into rolling foothills, finally reaching Albuquerque. As canyons and passes go, Tijeras Canyon is tame, allowing everyone coming into the city to enjoy the views. Before you get there, though, you come across the Mountain Lodge, a small motel at the base of Tijeras Canyon. The only thing left of the lodge, which burned and was subsequently razed, is this sign, but it is a classic motel sign, letting people know, if nothing else, that they are in the West.

We leave Tijeras Canyon still on the way to Albuquerque, a city that has been established for three hundred years, but before we get there, we pass through a watered-down version of another Dead Man's Curve. Before Interstate 40, there was a remarkably sharp curve here in the roadway with a remarkable number of accidents. The construction of Interstate 40 widened and straightened this strip, however, mitigating the danger. This Dead Man's Curve was a bit more intense than the Illinois one, since it saw higher-speed traffic.

Route 66 follows a mostly straight line through the city to Albuquerque's western edge. Over the years Route 66 slowly became Central Avenue and gradually developed. Little by little the original structures either disappeared or were repurposed as other businesses. Many of the motor lodges became apartments, and most have a general malaise about them. Here and there you can find traces of their old glory, though. One motor lodge still has the broken neon lighting along the upper wall and around some windows. It must have been spectacular back when it was all lit up. Early photographs show neon lights stretching up and down Central, er, Route 66, seemingly turning night into day, at

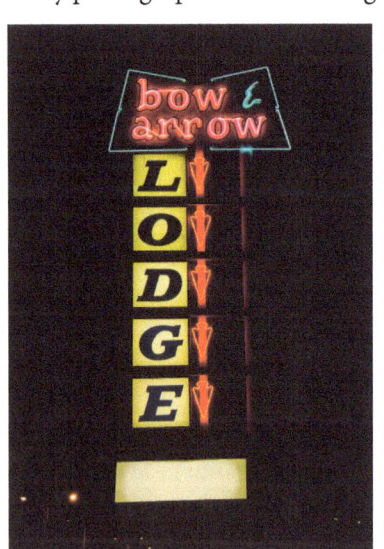

least for a little while. Albuquerque is not oblivious to its past and actively encourages businesses to maintain or restore their 66 heritage, allowing the stories of the Mother Road to continue finding new ears.

The Bow & Arrow Lodge sign is a classic one, simple and straight to the point. Literally. Arrows point straight at the entrance, leaving no doubt where to turn to stay the night.

The Pioneer Motel sign still advertises to passing motorists, although these days the nearby Interstate 40 siphons off much of the traffic. Still, despite needing quite a bit of work, the red, white, and blue of the sign is eye-catching.

The curtains went up for the Hiland Theater, along with its memorable sign, in 1950, and audience members have been thrilled ever since. The theater seats more than 1,000 people, so it is not a small place by any means, and one can only imagine what it was like in its heyday. It saw movies last in 1995 and was then converted to live theater, which closed in 2004. Since then, it has been taken over by National Dance Institute of New Mexico, which will keep the spirit of the theater alive. Fortunately this magnificent theater avoided its last curtain call.

The Zia Motor Lodge is one of the more famous motel courts in Albuquerque. Built in 1938, it was front and center during the golden years of Route 66. An old postcard from 1985 sums it up nicely: Air conditioned units, ceramic-tiled combination tub and shower, wall-to-wall carpeting, hot water heat, room phones, sun deck, and a patio. There is writing on the postcard, too, and the commentary is priceless: "This place is a beauty at nite[sic]. The trees are turning yellow. Have yellow lights on em. The front is green neon all around." It describes the Zia Motor aptly, although to be fair, it also describes many of the other motor courts of the day.

In 2003 a fire gutted the motel, leaving it a total loss. The City of Albuquerque demolished what was left, but it cannot destroy the memories the Zia Motor Lodge left behind.

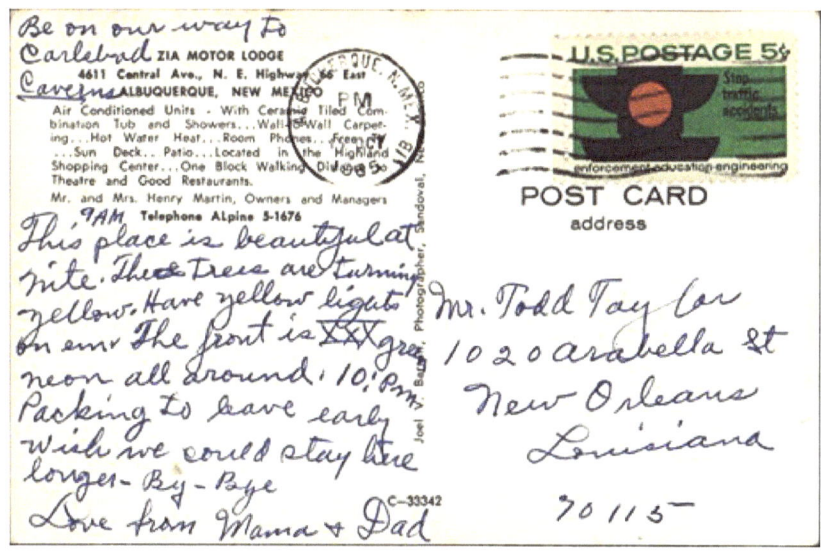

New Mexico 71

The De Anza Motor Lodge is another iconic motel and nearly suffered the same fate as the Zia Motor Lodge. Built in 1939 by S. D. Hambaugh and C. G. Wallace, the De Anza was one of the must-do stops in Albuquerque. The motel offered Zuni merchandise, courtesy of C. G. Wallace, making it an odd but effective combination of motor court and trading post. Early on, Wallace developed trading with the nearby Zuni Indians and capitalized on it through the Albuquerque area. The De Anza benefited from that association. Like the Zia Motor Lodge, the De Anza boasted air conditioning, telephones, and showers. The De Anza billed itself as ultramodern, which back then was accurate and impressive.

Today the De Anza has fallen on harder times and is no longer open for business. The property is in possession of the City of Albuquerque, which is making efforts to renovate and redevelop the property while retaining its legendary status.

The 66 Diner was originally Sam's Sixty Six Service, a Phillip's gas station. The diner now serves burgers and shakes and features a 1950s ambiance. Even the wait staff's uniforms are period correct. The neon-bathed building is a popular destination for a good meal.

When we head through downtown Albuquerque, we can stop and stand at the corner of Central Avenue, an east-west street, and 4th Street, a north-south one. Here is the only place along the entire route where Route 66 crosses itself. This impossible feat is the result of the massive alignment change previously mentioned. The original route went north through Santa Fe and then south through Albuquerque on 4th Street. When the route was realigned to be continuously east and west, it ran along Central and crossed 4th, thus this intersection is where the route crosses itself. Nothing here marks this anomaly, and it is just something you have to know.

The El Don Motel opened in 1946, although these days it is closed. The attention-grabbing sign captures our imagination and evokes the spirit of the Wild West.

The Monterey Motel has one of the more interesting neon signs, and what makes it unique is that it advertises itself as a non-smokers motel and has since the beginning. Even when smoking was something everyone did, this motel stood out. It has also stood the test of time and is still going strong. Coincidence? Maybe not.

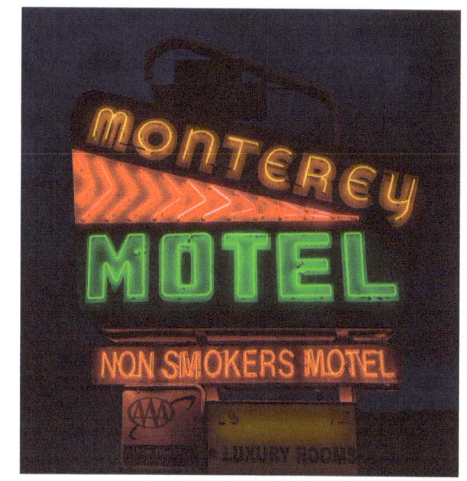

Opening in 1937 the El Vado Motel served weary travelers until 2008, an impressive run for this historic motor court. With thirty-two units and a gas station, it was made a perfect stopping place if you were entering or leaving Albuquerque. Using the Spanish Pueblo Revival style, the El Vado evoked the feel of Southwest Pueblos, and was an economic boon for Albuquerque.

A private developer, with help from the City of Albuquerque, purchased the property and redeveloped it. The redevelopment effort, completed in late 2017, retained the character of the original motor court. The El Vado continues to serve weary travelers.

We've not exhausted Albuquerque, but from this point until further west, only vague remnants and relics of the old route remain. Albuquerque is revitalizing Route 66, so perhaps one day we can expand this section, but for now it's time to motor down the highway. We continue to be California bound.

After Albuquerque we make a long, gentle ascent up Nine Mile Hill, a name perfectly given, as we leave the Rio Grande River valley. Cresting the hill we can see for miles upon miles, just short of forever, but we can't quite see California yet. The road, however, is straight and smooth, and before long we find ourselves in Budville at the old trading post.

Budville used to be a minor stop on the highway, serving as a general store, post office, and general "go-to" place. The doors have been closed for a good number of years now, so we'll keep moving.

New Mexico

The Acoma Curio Shop is another business long closed on this lonely stretch of Route 66, but once was a bustling place. Built before the Route 66 days, this small shop first served the immediate surrounding community and then highway travelers. For whatever reason, the building has a false front that reminds you of an old mining building. True to the name, the Acoma Curio Shop carried goods almost exclusively from the neighboring Acoma Indians.

We come to our second Whiting Brothers station, or at least the remains of one. Originally a gas station, motel, and most likely a café stood here. The concrete remains of the floors are the only thing left to tell the story, and if only they could talk, the story would be much more complete. At least a twenty-foot sign still marks the spot, worse for the wear, but standing tall.

We'll see more of the Whiting Brothers before we reach Santa Monica.

The Sands Motel in Grants has been around a while and has seen its share of guests, including Elvis and Priscilla Presley. Perhaps because it is in a larger city, it has managed to survive the universal downturn of Route 66, and it is still open for business. Better yet, its neon sign is lit at night as well.

The Sands Motel is technically not on the Mother Road and thus not a candidate for inclusion in *Route 66*; however, its sign is on Route 66, so we're splitting hairs. We'll include it because of the sign, which is a lovely example of 1960s-era advertising, with neon added. Best of all, it even has some rooms available tonight, unlike the Los Alamitos Motel down the street.

Feeding hungry diners since 1937, the Grants Café is another of the Route 66 eateries that keep going and going.

The Los Alamitos Motel sign is badly in need of repair. The motel itself is in need of, well, everything, since being leveled years ago. The sign, however, is classic and must have been quite eye-catching when it was lit. It is only a matter of time before the sign disappears, leaving no trace of the Los Alamitos.

Time to leave Grants and return to the open road.

A few miles outside of Grants we come to the small town of Bluewater, former home of the Bluewater Motel. The sign is another Route 66 classic and still looks good, despite the fact that the years have not been kind to it.

Bluewater has a long history, dating back into the late 1800s. Settled by ranchers and homesteaders, it was never a large town by any means and survived first because of its inhabitants, then the railroad, then Route 66, and then, well, not much. The Bluewater Motel was an excellent stopping point, and it saw a fair amount of business. The motel is closed now and is private property. Considering that the land is flat as a pancake for miles in every direction, this sign must have been a welcome beacon in the distance for the weary traveler. Today it is a beacon to the modern-day Route 66 tourist and still calls across the miles.

We finally enter Gallup, the last city in New Mexico, and our trek across this fascinating state is almost at its end. Before we leave New Mexico, though, we have a few more treasures to explore, including the Road Runner Motel.

The sign for the Road Runner Motel is another classic piece of advertising. With a slight nod to the Art-Deco style of the 1930s and heritage from the 1960s, this is a great-looking sign. It's full of colors and angles and shapes, and oh yes, a roadrunner. New Mexico has a healthy population of roadrunners, and it is nice to see them acknowledged with a motel.

The Desert Skies Motel sign is a collection of styles without actually adhering to one. It has some nice touches of neon and the classic 1960s type of lighted letters, all arranged mostly in a triangle. The sign shines into the night, the motel is open, and all in all, even after all these years, it is still inviting travelers to it. Opening in 1959, it listed "hi-fi music" as one of its amenities.

The Desert Skies is still accepting new reservations, a welcome change from too many of the "motels" we have visited.

The Arrowhead Lodge sign is another older sign in Gallup. The strip of Route 66 as you enter Gallup from the east has quite a few vintage and original signs from the late 1950s and early 1960s. Gallup celebrates Route 66 heritage, and when you drive through it, you might be looking at your calendar to reassure yourself of the current year.

No writings about Route 66 in New Mexico would be complete without mentioning the fabled Hotel El Rancho, home away from home for the movie stars.

Built in 1937, the Hotel El Rancho was designed to resemble a ranch. R. E. Griffith, the builder, did exceptionally well at meeting that goal. Even today, after all these years, looking at it makes you think of a ranch somewhere out in the Wild West. By good fortune, the areas surrounding Gallup were perfect for western movies. The stars needed a place to stay, and the El Rancho became the place to go. John Wayne is one of the more major stars to stay there, but he was in good company with Kirk Douglas, Ronald Reagan, and Katharine Hepburn. Excellent records of who stayed in what room exist, so today you can sleep where the stars did, although the mattresses have been replaced.

Even with all its star power, the El Rancho began to feel the effects of a fading Route 66, and the facility began to struggle until it closed in 1987. Adding insult to injury, the building was scheduled for demolition, and it looked like this icon of the movie stars was about to face its final act. In the nick of time, Armand Ortega bought the hotel. Armand couldn't bear to leave the El Rancho to its fate. Slowly and painstakingly he renovated it, and equally slowly and painstakingly, it came back to life.

Today the El Rancho shines brightly against the dark New Mexico skies, and the hotel is once again going strong. In fact it is best to make reservations. Who knows what future star will spend the night here?

Alas we say good night to New Mexico, and we head for the Arizona border, which is a couple of miles down the road.

Arizona

The Mother Road continues its headlong charge across Arizona. Here the land is wide and vast and the people few, giving a profound sense of solitude as you cruise beneath the azure skies. Arizona is full of surprises, too. You start on straight and smooth roads, yet you end up on some of the most treacherous portions that Route 66 has to offer.

Route 66 in eastern Arizona is a drive into the past, and in many places it is no more. Interstate 40 was laid on top of the original road, completely erasing it. Towns between the state line and Holbrook are few and far between. The tumbleweeds are at home here, and as pretty as the land is, it is barren of Route 66 artifacts and relics.

The abandoned Fort Courage complex, in Houck, a few miles past the state line, exemplifies the difficulty businesses on the Mother Road face, even when the interstate graces them with an exit. Perhaps it was just this exit that allowed Fort Courage to hang on, but in the end, time took its toll.

The concept was straightforward and ingenious: build a "fort" in the middle of the desert, name it like a real fort, and then wait for tourists to roll in. The concept worked and worked well, and young boys would hound their parents to stop and explore the structure. This place was a pure tourist trap, but one with a slightly different twist. A pancake house and coffeehouse were added to appease Mom and Dad as well as feed the now-hungry soldiers.

The cars whizz by too quickly, potential young soldiers don't heed the bugle call, and the complex is fading into the desert. It was a good run before Fort Courage finally closed its doors.

Right before we come to the town of Holbrook we find the Sahara Inn. Route 66 has many motifs along it, and calling back to the desert always adds to the charm. The camel is not the first we've seen, either. The topic of camels will come up shortly, and that will be the last time we have the opportunity to talk about camels.

The Pow Wow Trading Post in Holbrook used to be the Pow Wow Motel, where you could spend the night and peruse the associated rock and curio shop. Lately it converted to a rock shop only, and in the process changed the word Motel to Rocks on the sign. Interest in rocks is not what it used to be, and the sign now advertises a business that no longer exists. It remains an eye-catching sign.

As we motor through Holbrook, we come to a billboard with a question: "Have You Slept in a Wigwam Lately?" Luckily there happens to be a wigwam right next to the sign that we can, indeed, sleep in.

The Wigwam motels are an interesting story and one that can still involve you. Two of the concept motels survive along the route, one here in Holbrook, and the other in San Bernardino, California, although originally there were a total of seven across the United States. Designed by Frank Redford in the 1930s to resemble teepees, this idiosyncratic concept attracted attention, and attention means business. Frank was most interested in seeing people enjoy his wigwams and made licensing the idea as easy as possible.

Arizona   79

In the 1950s Chester Lewis bought a license and thus was born Wigwam Village #6 in Holbrook, which operated until 1974. Consisting of fifteen concrete teepees, the Wigwam Motel opened again in 1988, and yes, you can still sleep in a wigwam. We'll visit the other one as we wind down our journey.

Down the road from the Wigwam is the Plainsman Coffee Shop. Although the shop has long been closed, its sign still catches attention. Using a rifle as a signpost was a clever idea and reinforces the coffee shop's theme. Note that you can see the Wigwam Motel from here.

Now that we've purchased some rocks, slept in a wigwam, and had an excellent cup of coffee, we'll leave Holbrook and continue westward.

We'll stop briefly at the corner of Second Street and Kinsley in Winslow, Arizona, and enjoy the moment. Made famous by the Eagles song "Take It Easy," this is, at best, a corner. Still, it is a famous corner, and here we are. When we're finished standing on the corner, we'll mosey along.

Down the highway we come to the remnants of the Twin Arrows Trading Post. The outpost, operating from the early 1960s until more or less 1999, was a one-stop shop in the desert. It sold gas for both cars and trucks, had an authentic Valentine Diner, a café, and a curio shop, so you could find whatever you needed here. It was a bustling place and one of the locations on the road everyone seemed to stop at.

Little of it remains. The iconic twin arrows stand today, sliding into decay. The remaining shells of the buildings are frequent targets for vandals and thieves, who are making short work of what time does not.

Our next stop is in Williams, Arizona, at the long-gone El Rancho Motel. In its heyday, 1952, this sign would have been attractive and eye-catching. Alas, it continues to fade away, and it has been a long time since its neon lights were illuminated. For the curious, the El Rancho was green neon, and the rest was red. We're not likely to see it lit anytime soon.

The small town of Ash Fork served travelers passing through on Route 66, just like many other cities along the length of the Mother Road, and like its brethren, it suffered the same fate. Eventually businesses closed, and in most cases, that was the end of their story. This old Texaco station, however, has been repurposed into a modern-

day hair salon, which is not that unusual. What is unusual is that the salon called back to the good old days of Route 66 advertising, and for no reason other than to do it, placed a Desoto on the roof of the building. It's commendable to see the advertising spirit alive and well.

Oh, and in case you are wondering, the driver is none other than Elvis himself. Really. He must have checked out of the Sands and is now cruising the highway with us. We are in good company.

Outside of Ash Fork we find the longest surviving-segment of Route 66. Usually the interstate was built right next to, or on top of, the existing route and often made the highway into a frontage road. Here, however, Interstate 40 chose a different path, and the two diverge significantly for the rest of Arizona, leaving the existing route frozen in time. From here, we'll not see the interstate until Kingman, Arizona, quite a way down the highway.

This significant rerouting has posed a particularly difficult struggle for the towns along it, which is a shame, because they have much to offer. We'll explore all 158 miles of this segment and see what we can find.

Our first stop in Seligman is at the Stagecoach 66 Motel. Although the forty-room motel is still taking reservations, the sign is the interesting part. Originally built in the 1960s for the Bil-Mar-Den Motel, the sign has morphed over the years into its current form. The Betty Boop character was also a more recent addition to the sign. The sign is a great example of changing with the times, all to keep travelers coming in.

Opening in 1952, the Supai Motel has been in operation ever since. A restoration effort brought this classically styled sign back to life in 2006.

As we head down the road from Seligman, we encounter another set of Burma-Shave signs. Like before, these comprise witty sayings, ultimately extolling Burma-Shave. Unlike before, these re-creations suffer a fatal flaw: there never were any Burma-Shave signs in Arizona. Still, they are Burma-Shave signs, authentic or not.

While we roll down the empty highway, it's hard for us to miss Cavern Inn and Radiator Springs, and that is a good thing. Both are significant to us.

The Cavern Inn serves as a stop for the Grand Canyon Caverns. Although Route 66 doesn't go directly to the Grand Canyon, it does go near it, especially here. The Grand Canyon Caverns are enormous caves in the Grand Canyon. You will want to have a good night's rest before visiting them, though, and what better way than to stay here at the Cavern Inn?

When Route 66 was gravel in this location, it went right by the entrance of the caverns, although when it became a hard-surface road, its course moved a bit away. The inn has been in business since the late 1920s.

The Cavern Inn is not the only significant part of this complex, either. The Radiator Springs filling station and café featured prominently in the 2006 Disney/Pixar movie *Cars*. Radiator Springs is a fictional town made up by the movie, although there are similarly named cities such Baxter Springs in Kansas and Peach Springs here in Arizona.

This location inspired the Pixar artists, however, so now the filling station is known as Radiator Springs. As another bit of trivia, although the movie featured Tow Mater, a tow truck, and indeed a tow truck sits here at the newly named Radiator Springs, the original inspiration came from a tow truck now parked in Baxter Springs, Kansas.

Lest you think you can go as fast as you like, you might want to consider the possibility that an officer of the law might be waiting for you. As a case in point, the Radiator Springs Police Department has been known to lie in wait for unsuspecting motorists. Don't say you weren't warned.

A little farther down the road, in Truxton, we come to the Frontier Motel. This small nine-room motel and café built in the early 1950s served travelers on the busy road for quite a while. The lack of continued and reliable traffic forced it to close, a not-unfamiliar fate. In 2002 the National Park Service Corridor Preservation Program helped restore the aging sign, but in the intervening years, it has deteriorated and once again needs restoration.

Next to the door of the café is a small, weathered sign that reads Welcome Travelers. These signs were found all along the route, and for the weary or hungry motorist were a welcome relief. Not many of these signs can be found today, so it is always exciting when we see one.

The fictional town of Radiator Springs isn't the only law enforcement zone in these parts. An officer has been waiting for you at Hackberry, Arizona, as well, although by the look of things, he has been waiting for quite some time. Perhaps you don't need to worry too much in this case.

Hackberry is a small community that has always had a hard go of it. Initially a small mining community, it became a virtual ghost town by 1890 and remained obscure until the 1930s, when the Northside Grocery opened along the newly created Route 66. Even at that, Hackberry, aside from being a convenient stopping place, never grew any larger.

Next to the store an old Model T waits patiently to cruise the highway again. In the meantime, the elements have not been kind to it. This particular scene is quite famous and is often used to represent Route 66 in Arizona.

Today Hackberry is anything but obscure, and it is one of the iconic locations in Arizona. Better yet, it is open as a curio shop. The entire scene is like looking into a time capsule, since Hackberry hasn't changed much, if at all, over the years.

Not long after Hackberry, we roll into Kingman, Arizona, one of the larger cities on the route in Arizona. On the way in, we pass under Interstate 40, making it the first time we've seen the interstate in quite some time. Kingman has been a central part of Arizona history since the 1770s, when the Spanish explored the area. In 1857, Edward Beale made camp here, lending his name to local roads and even the Beale Hotel. To tie up a couple of loose ends we previously talked about, the Beale Expedition used camels to explore the area, so seeing a few camel motifs here and there along our journey makes sense.

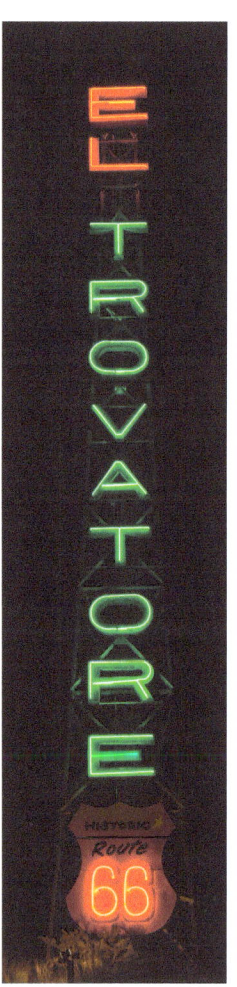

We're getting ahead of ourselves, however, and before we get to the Beale Hotel, we have a few stops to make, such as the Hill Top Motel.

Built in 1854, the Hill Top Motel has boasted from the beginning that it has the best view in Kingman. Before Kingman expanded, this was the case, and even today, one could argue that it is still true. The sign is bright and colorful, both in the daytime and, thanks to a restoration in 2002, at night as well. Its classic neon combination of red and green continues to light up the Arizona night, although it will need more work soon.

Down the hill from the Hill Top and well within sight of it is the El Trovatore. Built in 1939, and first an auto court, this motel still has rooms available, each with a different theme. What makes it stand out, however, is the tower-style neon sign visible almost everywhere. It makes you wonder if this is what the Hill Top meant when it said it has the best view in Kingman.

Down the road and at the bottom of the hill we find the restored Entering El Trovatore neon sign. Originally installed in 1936 to let motorists know they were coming into El Trovatore, the sign was taken down in the late 1940s when the alignment changed because of a new road. It sat in storage for more than seventy years, until it underwent restoration, was placed once again on Route 66, and re-lit. As many icons and businesses fade away, now and then one manages to make it back into the limelight, or in this case, neon light.

As we continue west, we come to the Arcadia Lodge, built in 1938. In the 1940s you could book a room here for $3.00, which included air conditioning. Today we would be beyond delighted with that rate! Over the years, especially in the 1960s, the property continued to expand, and it advertised itself as Spanish styling with landscaping. There were plans as late as the 1990s to continue the expansion, but it never materialized.

Meeting the fate of many of the early lodges and motels, the Arcadia has been converted into private apartments. At least it is still alive, and perhaps one day the expansion plans will be revived.

Our last stop in Kingman is the one we teased in the opening—Hotel Beale. Serving passengers of the Santa Fe Railroad since 1900, the hotel has long been a highlight of Kingman. In 1906 it was purchased by Tom Devine, the father of the famous actor Andy Devine, and it later served Route 66 travelers. Interestingly, street signs through Kingman mark Route 66 as Andy Devine Avenue, and the hotel is woven deeply into the fabric of Kingman.

Once we've checked out of the hotel, we plunge back into the desert, continuing to make our way toward California.

The drive out of Kingman is deceptively pleasant. At first the road runs straight through the desert, with nary a hint of what lies ahead. As the old roads do, it follows the contours of the land, so although you drive straight as an arrow, you also rise and fall into the small and sometimes not so small arroyos that crisscross your path. It is easy to be lulled into thinking that you will be in California in no time at all.

After a while, the road begins to rise gently, barely noticeable at first. Foot by foot you lift up and out of the valley, and if you look around, you notice that you can see a lot farther than you could a little while before. You'll also see Cool Springs, which means we need to stop. We'll return to the road in a moment.

Nestled in the foothills of the Black Mountains, the mountains we are about to transverse, we find the 1920s filling station of Cool Springs. When it first opened and this stretch of Route 66 was busy with travelers, Cool Springs had eight cabins, a café, and a bar. Journeyers were compelled to stop here in what seemed like a perfect location, and it was always a busy and happening place. Its ideal location turned out to be the exact opposite when a straighter alignment bypassed it in 1953, and the once-popular stop began its decline. Before it could ultimately grind to a halt, however, Cool Springs burned to the ground, leaving just the foundation. From there things went from bad to far worse.

The years took care of what the fire did not, and Cool Springs continued its deterioration. That is until the movie studios found it and decided it would make an excellent movie location. The 1991 film *Universal Soldier* built a wooden frame around the remaining foundation and used the location in the movie. At the end of the story, Cool Springs was blown to smithereens, once again obliterating it. This final act was, naturally enough, the bitter end for Cool Springs.

What about now? How is it that we are stopping at Cool Springs?

Some people are determined to bring back the spirit of the Mother Road. They refurbish and rehabilitate old properties to give them life and purpose again. Others do what they can to preserve a property as it stands, and then there are folks like Ned Leuchtner, who decided to rebuild Cool Springs one rock at a time after he fell in love with the location and history. He started in 2001 and completed the rebuild in 2004. Working from old photographs and local knowledge, Ned painstakingly resurrected Cool Springs, once again bringing it back to life.

Refreshed, we head back down the highway into the teeth of the Black Mountains.

From here the road rises harrowingly into the Black Mountains, beginning one of the most famous, or infamous, if you prefer, stretches of the entire highway. The twisting, winding, treacherous path picks its way up and through the mountain pass, and in the early days, this portion of the road was extremely dangerous. In the days of the Model T, there were no assurances you would make it through this section, and some did not. Some motorists hired local drivers to guide their cars through this area, and with good reason. Hairpin curves, blind corners, steep drop-offs, and steep grades all combined to make a truly hair-raising experience. Remember, the Mother Road followed the contours of the land.

In the flat farmland of Illinois, this plan is idyllic. In the Black Mountains of Arizona, this is truly terrifying. The road continues upward, and with every passing moment, it finds a new way to scare the daylights out of you.

Eventually the road crests at Sitgreaves Pass, where you can stop, breathe, and once your heart stops racing, enjoy the panoramic views. Once, long ago, there was a convenient filling station here, but those days are long gone. All that remains is the road down. With a last check of the brakes, it is time to begin the headlong plunge down the mountains, and if all goes well, arrive in Oatman.

Oatman, Arizona, was once a thriving mining community. Nestled in isolation in the Black Mountains we barely managed to make it through, Oatman is as rugged as they come.

Founded in the early 1900s, Oatman has its roots as a mining town. The mountains were ideal for mining gold, and like many mining communities, it lived at the whims of the mines, and eventually the mines played out. Had it not been for Route 66 passing right through it, Oatman would have gone the way of countless other, mostly forgotten, mining towns. As it happened, though, Route 66 kept Oatman alive until 1953, when the alignment was changed to pass through Yucca, bypassing this stretch of road. Oatman faced extinction.

Living up to its rough-and-tumble image, the town somehow managed to survive. Although it is more of a tourist town than anything else, its streets are as crowded as ever, but instead of with grizzled old miners, with tourists shopping for trinkets in the true Route 66 fashion.

The White Bird Trading Post as we enter Oatman gives us an excellent glimpse of how it looked in the very early days of the Mother Road. It has a few extra gas signs that it has collected over the years, but otherwise it looks much the same.

From Oatman we head through the western foothills, a far more gentle affair than a few miles back, making our way over the Colorado River and finally into California.

California

With a final, arduous push across the desolate Mojave Desert, we are within reach of our destination: Santa Monica. With every passing mile, our excitement builds, and as we motor through the desert, then the gently rolling hills, and then the last easy miles, we become more and more excited. Finally, after 2,448, miles we reach our destination.

As a whole, California, like its seven other brethren states, continues to remember and keep Route 66 alive. Route 66 faces the twin challenges of the Mojave Desert and development, however, both of which have taken a significant toll.

The Mother Road cuts across the arid and treacherous Mojave, where temperatures soar to over 120 degrees in the summer months, and the nights can dip below zero in winter. When traffic switched to the new Interstate 40, Route 66 went into an immediate decline. Although a few places lingered on in the desert, many business owners abandoned their enterprises. Little of these establishments remain, but we'll visit of few to pay homage.

Farther west, the city of Los Angeles, as well as its myriad suburbs, quickly overwhelmed Route 66. As in the previous larger cities, the land was too valuable to abandon, so old motels, gas stations, and curio shops, among others, were razed to make way for more modern building and business.

Even though Route 66, maintaincd as a signed route, still exists today, it looks far different than it did in the past.

Our first stop in California is Needles, just inside the border. Needles was never a large town, and in its heyday served the travelers of the National Old Trails Highway and later Route 66. Even the interstate couldn't prevent the overall decline when it came through, and today Needles struggles on while its nearby neighbors Laughlin and Bullhead City have grown exponentially.

The fact that Needles is on the smaller side, though, doesn't mean it is devoid of the arts. Opened in 1930 and built by the Masonic Lodge, the Needles Theater had seven hundred seats and entertained people until 1992, when the building caught fire. Since then the building has struggled, with renovations planned, but not completed. At least the marquee is lit and welcoming us to Needles.

From Needles, Route 66 slices across the Mojave Desert, making its way to Barstow. The drive was stressful, especially on the earlier cars, which didn't fare well in the heat. Small towns, and especially service stations, dotted the landscape, but today most of those are nearly unrecognizable ruins. To further complicate the present-day drive, bridges along the route are prone to washing out, and in the best case, in need of serious repair. The California Department of Transportation maintains them, but as you can imagine, they are not high on the list of priorities. Be that as it may, we eventually make our way just past Amboy to the Roadrunner's Retreat.

The sign before us used to be an attention-getting neon sign. Perched on a slight rise, it was visible for miles upon miles and beckoned travelers. The motel, restaurant, and Standard Oil station, all built in 1932, served as an outpost and stopping point for travelers until 1995, when it finally surrendered to the inevitable. In the intervening years there have been some plans, or perhaps more accurately hopes, to restore the complex. Maybe one day it will once again light the nighttime desert sky.

Roadrunner's Retreat with the Marble Mountains and Old Woman Mountains in the distance, especially in the fading sun of the late afternoon, creates a spectacular sight. With Route 66 running into the distant mountains, this scene makes a powerful impact.

But we must move on!

Our next stop is in Ludlow, a town barely hanging on. We first encounter a building that's crumbling into ruins, which gives an excellent example of abandoning a structure. It won't be too many years before the building collapses on itself, leaving only the metal frame of what used to be a sign, to remind anyone that something was once here.

A short distance away is the old Ludlow Café and an old filling station, both long disused. The Ludlow Fire Department has chosen to use the awning as protection for its truck, but from the looks of things, it is best that you not call the department in case of fire.

California   93

In the town of Newberry Springs we find Dry Creek Station, an old Whiting Brothers facility. Built in 1951, it pumped gas until the mid-1990s and has remained empty ever since. A café also used to be here, but it is slowly fading into the desert.

All that's left of the Henning Motel is the sign. Time and the elements are doing their best to remove the sign, but it is a sturdy metal one, and so far has resisted their efforts as best as it can. In the background is Bagdad Café. The Bagdad Café used to be known as the Sidewinder Café, but it had a sign reading Bagdad Cafe installed on it for the 1988 movie of the same name. Rather than restore the original signage, the café kept the new name. Route 66 businesses are practical, if nothing else.

At last we reach the end of the long stretch through the Mojave Desert and arrive safely in Barstow, California, where motels and services await us. We'll make a quick stop, and keep moving since we don't have far to go.

First up is the Stardust Inn, which has been hosting travelers since the earliest days of Route 66. The classic sign would remind one of Las Vegas, Nevada, perhaps intentionally.

This modern-day view of Barstow could have been made any time in the last fifty years, since not much has changed since then. In the foreground is the Torches Motel, with a guest just leaving, and in the background is the Route 66 Motel.

A short distance from Barstow is Helendale and the remains of Watson's Richfield Station, which was a filling station and repair shop. It served both Route 66 and later Interstate 15.

Route 66 has had its share of businesses that have struggled and ultimately not made it; however, now and then a new entity springs up along the road. In rare cases, it is one such as Elmer's Bottle Tree Ranch. Even though this is, in Route 66 terms, brand new, it is still a worthy mention.

Mere words are difficult to describe the Bottle Tree Ranch, so the photograph will have to bear the weight. It has more than two hundred "trees," or more accurately, bottle holders, with each bottle holder hosting more or less thirty-two bottles. Conservatively 6,400 bottles adorn the ranch, and it will likely continue growing. Scattered among the bottle trees are various artifacts such as signs, old bicycles, and unidentifiable small objects.

Elmer's Bottle Tree Ranch keeps alive the spirit and tradition of the best stops on Route 66, and for a declining highway, it is inspiring that folks such as Elmer Long keep creating new treasures along the Mother Road.

As we arrive in Victorville we find ourselves at Emma Jean's Holland Burger Café, which is home to the famous Brian Burger, at least according to the signage. Emma Jean's began flipping burgers in 1947 and is still in business. It is a genuine Mom & Pop operation, and even though Route 66 is in decline, Emma Jean's appears to be here to stay.

The New Corral Motel in Victorville has an attention-grabbing sign. The rearing stallion is striking and still calls to motorists to stay the night. The New Corral Motel has been open since 1947, and thanks to recent renovations, plans to remain that way.

From here Route 66 heads up and over Cajon Pass at Cajon Summit. At 3,776 feet, this elevation is the highest we'll be, as from here it is all downhill to Santa Monica and the Pacific Ocean. As we head down the pass, we encounter the outskirts of the greater Los Angeles area.

Before we arrive in Los Angeles proper, however, we come across this lonely Eat sign. As might be expected, there is nowhere anymore to sit down for a meal, but the sign tells us this wasn't always the case.

Our first significant stop after Cajon Pass is Wigwam Motel #7 in San Bernardino, California. Built in 1949 and consisting of nineteen teepees, this motel is much the same as the one where we stayed earlier in Holbrook, Arizona. Like the previous Wig-Wam, the motel is open for business.

In the mid-1990s this motel was in a state of severe decline and deep jeopardy. It had developed a seedy reputation, so few people wanted to stay there. It seemed that it might finally close its doors, because the land was worth more than the buildings. Kumar Patel, a lifelong fan of Route 66, purchased and faithfully restored the property, once again making it a viable place to stop.

These iconic motels serve not only as a beautiful place to spend the night but also remind us of the glory days of roadside attractions.

We head off again, making our way due west. We're not far away from the end now.

The 1950s Motel El Rey in Rialto still advertises color TV by RCA, although we assume that all TVs are color these days. It is nice to see the old sign still in use.

Down the road in Fontana is one of the few remaining Bono's Historic Orange stands. The orange-shaped and orange-colored stand sells orange and lemonade drinks. Originally built in 1936, this stand was moved to its current location in the late 1990s and has been serving drinks ever since. Back in the heyday, these stands were ubiquitous throughout this area.

The Cucamonga Service Station in Rancho Cucamonga is one of the few historical sites left in this area. Fully restored in 2015, complete with a new yellow color scheme, it is now open as a visitors center and museum. The station is more than one hundred years old, and it is lucky to have survived long enough to be restored.

The 1920s Golden Spur restaurant in Glendora has long been a staple of the area and Route 66. The Golden Spur started out as a burger stand that served horseback riders. It transformed itself into a more refined restaurant and a popular place for locals. The sign, dating from the 1950s, is classic Americana. The restaurant, even though it has outgrown its humble roots, proudly keeps the sign and remembers its heritage.

California

It has been a while—since Missouri, in fact—that we've seen a drive-in theater, and we can't end our journey without seeing one more. The Azusa Foothill Drive-In Theatre in Asuza fills the bill nicely. Opening in 1961, its original capacity was 1,510 cars, making it one of the larger drive-in theaters anywhere. The drive-in showed its last movie in December 2001.

The Los Angeles Conservancy says that the Azusa Foothill Drive-In is the last remaining drive-in theater on Route 66 west of Oklahoma, a claim we can readily verify, since we just came that way. Although the drive-in theater screen was demolished, the marquee will luckily be preserved for future generations.

Route 66 has been long and straight from San Bernardino up until this point. From here to Santa Monica, the route twists and turns, and in many cases, disappears altogether. We'll pick our way along it as best as we can, stopping at a few more places. Although California is doing its best to preserve this portion of Route 66, the rapid pace of modern development has swallowed the venerated highway.

In Monrovia we find an early alignment of Route 66 making a small south-to-north jog through a neighborhood. Here, like we saw back east but haven't seen since, is a gas station, this time a Flying A, nestled in a community. The station features classic Spanish style.

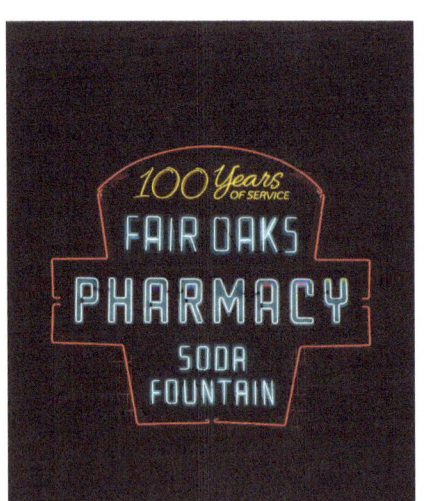

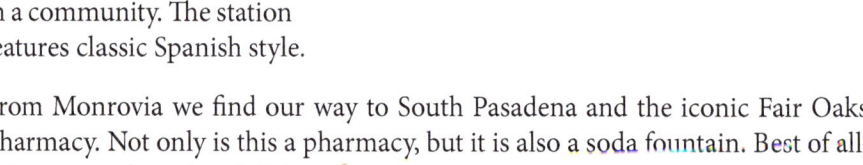

From Monrovia we find our way to South Pasadena and the iconic Fair Oaks Pharmacy. Not only is this a pharmacy, but it is also a soda fountain. Best of all, it is open and serving delicious food.

First opening its doors as the South Pasadena Pharmacy in 1915, it became the Raymond Pharmacy in the 1920s. In the process it also became a favorite stop on Route 66. Unlike what happened to so many of the other soda fountains, the owners completely restored it in the early 1990s, and today it continues to be a popular and important part of the neighborhood, not to mention of Route 66.

From South Pasadena it is a short drive to Santa Monica Pier and the sign we have been seeking. It reads simply End of Trail, and so it is. We've reached our destination, and before us stretches the Pacific Ocean.

The sign on the pier is a far cry from the one we saw at the very beginning of our journey. The city of Chicago grew up around it, swallowing both the sign and Route 66. Here nothing except the endless ocean stretches ahead of us at the end of the route, a fitting end for our journey. A few steps ahead of us is Santa Monica Pier and the end of the day, a perfect way for us to conclude.

But in true Route 66 fashion, there is just a little bit more to our story.

Much of the story of Route 66 is that of marketing. Signs were made to lure travelers in, and they became bigger, brighter, and bolder over the years. They used neon, which created an endless row of lights in the cities, in the hopes of enticing patrons. Businesses invented new ways to advertise, all in the name of competition, and as we've seen, countless examples of these ploys remain. Why, then, should our ending sign be any different?

The official, and seldom noted, end of Route 66 is at the corner of Olympic Boulevard and Lincoln Boulevard in Santa Monica, which is not Santa Monica Pier. Today, and even yesterday, this intersection is entirely unremarkable. When the highway was decommissioned in 1985, the intersection became just another intersection in the busy town of Santa Monica.

An enterprising trade group based on Santa Monica Pier recognized the value of having Route 66 "end" on the pier itself. Since the Department of Transportation officially decommissioned the route, there was no official way to say this could not be the case. Accordingly, the group erected the sign we see above on Santa Monica Pier, and without anyone realizing it, the end was moved a couple of blocks to the west. The trade group was correct in its assumption, and this marker helped drive additional traffic onto the pier and into the shops. These days, the general assumption is that Route 66 officially ends on Santa Monica Pier, and really, why not? It represents perfectly the spirit of Route 66.

Epilogue

Creating this work was a deeply moving experience and something I will treasure forever. When I first started this project, I wasn't quite sure what to expect. Being fortunate enough to live only a few miles from Route 66, I had traveled along small portions of it for years, always wondering "what if…?" Finally I was able to answer that question, and in a big way.

My partner, Mary Beth, and I traveled the highway several times over to create Route 66. Along the way we met some extraordinary people, without whom this work would not be the same.

Among countless examples, a few stand out, in no particular order.

When we visited the Fair Oaks Pharmacy, its neon sign was dark. During our meal, I asked about it. As it turns out, it was supposed to have been on, but a power outage messed up its timer. The staff called several people, after 6:00 p.m. on a Saturday night, mind you, to get the sign working. Finally, after quite a bit of effort, the staff succeeded, so that I could photograph the sign.

We visited Gay Parita close to sundown. I was doing my best to photograph it in the fading light, when Barb, the daughter of Gary Turner, saw me. As quick as could be, she opened everything up and turned on all the lights. While I was photographing, we all chatted, and she shared some of her stories with us. We ended up sitting on the front porch of the station as the sun finally set, watching the traffic breeze past. Eventually she asked if we had a place to stay. When I told her we didn't, she picked up the phone and called Boots Court and made sure it had a room for us. I headed there, thinking it was exactly how it has always been on the Mother Road, where friendliness and service are a way of life. When we arrived at Boots Court, the clerk was expecting us and greeted us by name, even though we had never met. Tired from a long day, we walked into a room frozen in time at 1949 with a radio softly playing period music. It was a surreal experience that I will long cherish. For a while, I lost track of what year it was.

At Roadrunner's Retreat waiting for the perfect golden rays of the late afternoon sun, I was deeply struck by the history of the place. I could hear cars whizzing by, although mine was the only vehicle driving that segment the entire day. I could see the trucks pulling into the station to fuel up, and I could hear, plain as day, the laughter spilling out of the long-gone café. While standing there, looking down the road toward the distant mountains, I felt I was a part of the Mother Road and its history. For that reason, Roadrunner's Retreat became the cover image of Route 66. I knew it would be the cover image from the moment I made the photograph.

The sense of wonderment and anticipation that I felt when I photographed the Begin Route 66 sign in Chicago was matched only by the same feelings, plus a tinge of regret, when I photographed the End of Trail sign in Santa Monica. Through all 2,448 miles, those feelings never left me.

Some experiences were, alas, not the best. In Gallup, New Mexico, teenagers yelled at me as they drove by. Miscreants surpassed that behavior a month later when someone threw a drink at me from a car. Luckily it didn't hit me, but it did leave me bewildered.

While I was photographing a café I shall not name, a couple walked toward us loudly arguing. As the couple passed us, they told us that they were just regular people and were OK. Paying them little attention, for loud people and bickering couples are not unusual when photographing on the streets, I was friendly and continued making my photograph. A few moments later we moved to the other side of the café, and lo and behold, we encountered the couple again. They surprised us, however, when they flashed their badges. It turns out they were setting up a bait car to catch car thieves. The loud arguing and walking away was the setup, nothing more. All of us stood and chatted about Route 66 while they kept an eye on the car. Luckily everyone was good that night, and the police didn't have to spring into action.

I could go on, but you get the idea. By and large, people were friendly and helpful. They shared their stories; they helped me by making sure I knew the proper history. They pointed me in the right direction, too, although some tried to tell me a tall tale. For all I know, they succeeded. Of the diners and establishments that have been open since the early days, all I can say is that there is a reason they are still open. The food is darn good.

The Mother Road is compelling and irresistible. Once I started photographing and documenting its stories, I found myself completely hooked. *Route 66* began as a small project but quickly grew into something far larger. It took on a life of its own as I brought the stories to life.

I know I have touched on only part of the stories out there, and more are out there, waiting for me.

To you, dear reader, thank you for taking this journey with me as we traveled down the Mother Road, Route 66.

About the Author

The sun sleeps on, not even thinking about rising yet. David, already standing out in a cold, wet field, waits for the sun and the wildlife to come alive. Seemingly the last place anyone else would want to be, this field springs to life with the dawn, and so does David's camera. Only the shot matters, in spite of toes threatening to move to the equator and fingers looking for a cup of coffee instead of wanting to hold the camera. He waits for exactly the right moment and then ... click. He has it.

David Schneider, a nature and wildlife photographer, focuses on bringing alive each scene and creature his camera sees. With a unique point of view and style, his prints capture the color, beauty, and soul of his subjects. His affinity for nature extends into the scenic arena as well. His landscapes bring out the incredible emotion, beauty, and grandeur of the Southwest and beyond; his photographs will take you from the tops of misty mountains to the shifting sands of the deep desert, letting you always be in the moment.

David lives in Tijeras, New Mexico, just outside of the Cibola National Forest. He prefers to be outside whenever possible, in his "studio"—the great outdoors. He believes in being one with nature, and not a day goes by that he doesn't find something new to be amazed and delighted by. David has had a lifelong interest in photography and nature, and his passions combine, providing arresting photographs for everyone.

Photo by M.B. McClean

www.ingramcontent.com/pod-product-compliance
Lightning Source LLC
Chambersburg PA
CBHW041551220426
43666CB00002B/31